DOLLIS JUNIOR SCHOOL
— A HISTORY —

DOLLIS
JUNIOR
SCHOOL

DOLLIS JUNIOR SCHOOL
— A HISTORY —

GLENN A. STEPPLER

TEMPUS

For Anna

Glenn A. Steppler lives in Mill Hill, and has been a governor at Dollis Junior School since 1999. His daughter, Anna, attended the school from 1998 to 2002, making her a most useful source of 'inside' information!

'I am proud to have had the honour to have been the first Head Teacher of the school. I trust the school will go from strength to strength and that all associated with the name Dollis will be proud of such association.'

Harry Bryant's first report as headteacher, Dollis Junior School, 2 February 1954

First published 2007

Tempus Publishing
Cirencester Road, Chalford,
Stroud, Gloucestershire, GL6 8PE
www.tempus-publishing.com

Tempus Publishing is an imprint of NPI Media Group

British Library Cataloguing in Publication Data.
A catalogue record for this book is available from the British Library.

ISBN 978 0 7524 4474 1

Typesetting and origination by NPI Media Group
Printed in Great Britain

CONTENTS

PREFACE

Writing a history is a largely solitary endeavour, but it is always a pleasure to acknowledge those who have answered questions and offered assistance along the way. At Dollis Junior School itself I would like to mention Jenny Bond, Ann Bull, Victoria Cleary, Dave Hallett, Matthew Heasman, Carol Jeffery, Maurice Markwell, Kathryn Morrell and Alison Sharpe. Thanks, too, must go to those former pupils who shared their memories of the school, in the school reunion room during the 2002 Summer Fête.

David Burns, and his successor Colin Dowland have both given support to this project, and special thanks must go to Androulla Alexander who undertook the production of a typescript that has seen many alterations and amendments.

At Dollis Infants School, the headteacher, Miss McGoldrick must be thanked for making available records kept at that school, while Gary Carney kindly assisted in answering several queries.

This history has been put together from many disparate sources, as indicated in the Bibliography. Many of the items from the school itself only became available in bits and pieces over a very extended period of time, access often being extremely difficult. Despite repeated requests to see the school log books from the 1980s to 1990s, these were never made available, and were taken away by Derek Heasman when he left the school in July 2004. Thanks, however, to the efforts of the former deputy headteacher, Matthew Heasman, a large cache of *School News* from this period did eventually become available.

Dollis in the Past

FIFTY YEARS AGO

BRITAIN IN 1952

Dollis Junior School opened in 1952. But what was Britain like fifty years ago? Following Labour's defeat at the polls, Winston Churchill was again prime minister. It was just over six years since Britain had emerged from the storms of a terrible war, and the effects of wartime austerely lingered still. Although the rationing of clothes, petrol and soap were no more, that on food (including sweets) remained. But things were getting better. In February wartime ID cards were abolished, in July the new NHS celebrated its fourth birthday and in October tea rationing came to an end. Shopkeepers served you from behind their counters, but the idea of self-service shopping had made an appearance. Britain's first supermarket, a Co-op in East London, was now four years old – and more recently a certain J. Sainsbury had opened a purpose-built supermarket in Croydon. There was even such a thing as a 'launderette', promising a much easier washday for mother – even men could use it, the attendant (female) would show them how!

New cars were expensive and in short supply. Old ones were kept going, too often with little regard to efficiency or safety. Driving instruction was haphazard and vehicles were not subject to mandatory inspection. The zebra crossing had been introduced the previous October. The general idea, though, was to keep the traffic flowing, removing any pedestrian obstructions where necessary. As yet there were no motorways – and in July London's last tram ran for the last time.

Radio and cinema were the principal sources of entertainment and although television was not new (public broadcasting had started in 1936) the 'box' was rare enough to still be something of a status symbol. If you were very lucky a relative or a neighbour might have one – but it was BBC only, and only in black and white. For all ages live entertainments were an important part of leisure time. Football drew its crowds, but a new Entertainment Tax threatened to drive up ticket prices to unheard-of levels – even to 2s a match! Consideration was being given to increasing the maximum player's wage of £20 a week, while there were also plans to cap players' transfer fees at £15,000. It had been almost twenty years since England had last won the Ashes – surely it was time for a change?

Clothes were looking brighter and smoking was fashionable. Women were wearing nylons – the new fabric had now been widely accepted for stockings, and even for underwear and blouses. Teenage girls wore skirts and dresses. Tight jeans and rock music would not reach Britain for several more years, but in November charts for pop-single records were published for the first time. In the City, gents still wore the bowler hat, and it had been going strong for over 100 years. Children enjoyed stories by Enid Blyton, and read avidly the *Adventures of Biggles*. Girls played with dolls and boys built cranes and lorries from Meccano sets. In Oxford C.S. Lewis was continuing to write and publish his *Narnia* stories, while his friend J.R.R. Tolkien was polishing up the final draft of his *The Lord of the Rings*.

Society was certain of its moral code, of the rules of social etiquette and of proper behaviour. Both the dance halls *and* the churches were full. One did not trade on a Sunday. Gambling was frowned upon and treated accordingly by magistrates. Women, like children, had their place, and for the former it did not put them on an equal footing with men, a point made clear should they leave the home for the workplace.

For Britain's young men, military conscription remained a fact of life. Britain and the Soviet Union (still in Stalin's grasp) viewed each other with mutual suspicion and hostility. In Korea and in Malaya British soldiers were fighting communists, while in Egypt and Kenya, Britain's continuing status as a colonial power brought her into further conflicts. In February, Churchill announced that Britain too had the atom bomb – and the fear of nuclear war was underscored by the Government's call for civil defence volunteers and a reactivation of the Home Guard. The close of the year brought immediate sorrow to many Londoners – an unprecedented Great Smog settled on the city and caused an estimated toll in related deaths, now put as high as 12,000. It led finally to the Clean Air Act of 1956.

Yet the event which stuck most in the public memory was the death of King George VI. The King died in February, aged only fifty-six. But if Britons had lost a much loved king, they had also gained a beautiful young queen. Dollis Junior School opened at the end of April, and in early May, while children and teachers were settling in, their new queen, Elizabeth II, was doing the same in her new residence at Buckingham Palace – and 1953 would be a year to look forward to. There was to be a royal coronation!

NEW HOUSES AND ... CHILDREN!

Both the present-day Dollis Junior and Dollis Infant Schools trace their origin back to the great period of council-estate building in the then Borough of Hendon in the 1920s and 1930s. The borough was experiencing a population explosion which was turning its centuries-old farmland into suburban estates. From 1931 to 1939 alone, it grew from 115,000 to 170,000. In 1936, while making plans for 'the Corporation's Housing Scheme at Dole Street', in Mill Hill East, an area of about 6 acres was laid aside for the construction of an elementary school. Indeed it was intended there would be sufficient land for two schools, as it was foreseen that there might come a time when the number of local children would require a second school to be built alongside the first. Construction began in May 1938 and in May 1939 the 'Dole Street (soon 'Dollis') Council Junior and Infant School' was opened. As the name indicates it had both a junior and an infant department – with nursery provision as well. In all there was accommodation for 440 junior and infant children (including not more than forty in a nursery classroom). On its first day it enrolled 300 children.

The outbreak of war that autumn, however, not only disrupted lessons but also derailed the plans of both the Borough's Housing Committee and its Education Committee. The general school population fell during the war years, but from 1942 the birth rate in Britain began to soar. With the end of the war the borough's population began to increase, rising by 16,000 between 1945 and 1951. Energy was turned into building new houses and this, coupled with a high birth rate soon put great pressure on local schools. Moreover, the 1944 Education Act had committed the Government to a large-scale programme of educational building. The Borough of Hendon's Education Committee (placed under the authority of Middlesex County Council since 1944), hoped to see a new school for 300 juniors to be erected on the Dollis site, included in Middlesex's Educational Building Programme of 1947/48. To local people the construction of new houses in the Mill Hill East area made this 'a matter of urgency', but the Middlesex County Council was at first unable to win approval for the new school from the Ministry of

Education. New Government criteria for post-war building projects proved a stumbling block. The construction of some 300 new houses, however, continued apace, and to alleviate the expected overcrowding which would result from the increase in the number of local school children, the county council was at least able to secure approval for two prefabricated classrooms, to be erected at Dollis under the Government's HORSA (Hutting Operation for the Raising of the School Leaving Age) scheme. Their construction began in September 1947, but the work dragged on into the following April, when the intervention of the borough's education officer finally pushed them to a conclusion. The delay in finishing the new classrooms was annoying, but in June (1948), when they were officially handed over to borough's education officer, they were already in need of 'minor repairs' – to the roof, the lights, etc – all duly noted in the presence of the borough surveyor and his guests, several officials from the Ministry of Works!

The HORSA hut, with its two classrooms, was not a final solution. In January 1946 the Dollis Junior and Infant School had reported 421 children on its rolls – a number well within its planned capacity. In May 1947, however, the headteacher noted that the roll was up to 434, and the following May (1948), when the two new classrooms were finally occupied, the Dollis roll stood at 510. But the press of numbers did not relent. By the spring of 1949 the roll was over 530 and at the start of the autumn term it stood at 540. Provision for a new junior school on the Dollis site was again inserted in the county's proposal for the educational building programme of 1949, and this time it won acceptance, though the formal approval of the Ministry of Education was still not received for some time to come.

PLANNERS, BUILDERS, TEACHERS AND CHILDREN

Planning for the new junior school was undertaken by Middlesex County Council, and in April 1949 the council approved an estimated expenditure of £86,080 for a new two-form entry school for 320 junior boys and girls, to be built at the existing site of the Dollis Junior and Infant School. As the original site would need to be extended, the Borough of Hendon was asked to transfer the additional land required for the new school to the county council. By May the county architect had completed his preliminary plans for the new school, and in November 1949 tenders were invited. A month later a tender from H. Pickrill Ltd for £79,000 was accepted, but it was only in the following January (1950) that the formal approval for the project was received from the Ministry of Education. The county architect was then told to proceed with the work as soon as possible, and in the spring of 1950 construction finally began.

The classroom blocks were begun first, and in air of optimism it was suggested that some of the classrooms would be ready for occupation as early as that autumn (1950). It was a prediction that soon went awry, blown off course by international crisis and rising costs at home, with labour and material shortages, and especially by difficulties in securing steel for new construction work. Most of the schools begun in 1948 and even some of those started in 1947 were still under construction, while the new Dollis Junior School was itself only one of thirty-one new schools to be built in Middlesex under the 1949 programme. It was not until the autumn of 1952 (when the administration block and the dining halls were finished) that the school was finally completed, and only in the autumn of 1951, when the school was reported to be 'nearing completion', that it was possible to actually use any of the new school's classrooms.

Teachers and children in the old school had endured an uncomfortably crowded building where, for more than three and a half years, the hall had done extra duty as both a classroom and a dining area. The moment when some of the classrooms in the new school could actually be used had been long awaited. On 7 September (1951) that moment finally arrived when, at the end of the first week of the new autumn term, Mr Kitson's class of forty-eight juniors (Form 2A) moved from the hall of the old school into a freshly finished classroom in the new school. The departure of Mr Kitson's class from the old school made its hall available once more for singing, dancing and PT lessons, and made mealtimes much easier too!

Academic life began in the new junior school with the builders still at work. A temporary partition separated those classrooms which were in use from the main, unfinished, corridor and from the noise of hammer and saw in other parts of the school (principally the administrative block, hall and kitchen) still under construction. The classrooms had to be heated with portable oil stoves, and at first the only available lavatories and cloakrooms were still in the old school. Mr Kitson's children were the new school's first occupants, but at the beginning of October a second classroom in the new school was brought into use, with children needing special help in reading, and others doing remedial exercises being taken there for lessons. In December plans were made to reorganise Dollis's 324 juniors into eight classes (from the existing seven), and to occupy more of the new school's classrooms after the Christmas break. The furniture of a further three junior classes was moved into the new school over the Christmas holiday and it was intended that when the school reopened on 9 January (1952), there would be altogether four junior classes in the new school, another two would continue in the HORSA hut, and two more would remain in the old school building.

As the four classes in the new school would be without proper cloakrooms, they would be given access to six of the new classrooms, two of which would serve as temporary cloakrooms, the children piling their overcoats, scarves, hats and bags on some fifty of the old school's worst desks, moved into the new school for that purpose. The builders and decorators continued their work. A brief glimpse of the activity can be gleaned from a note made in mid-March 1952 of the men then busily employed bringing the project to a conclusion. A site foreman watched over the efforts of some nineteen labourers, four bricklayers, one bricklayer's apprentice, two carpenters, one plumber, seven plasterers, two plasterer's apprentices, three painters, two electricians, one scaffolding man, three roofing men and six heating men. On 10 April the new kitchen (to serve both juniors and infants) was ready for use, just in time to serve meals during the Easter break, for it was then still the practice of the School Meals Service to provide local children with midday meals during school holidays. The dining halls, however, were only available in the autumn, 'early in the Christmas Term'.

By January 1952 then, half of the juniors were installed in the new junior school building, and the following month the Hendon Education Committee interviewed candidates for the post of headteacher at the new Dollis Junior School. Whereas at the start of September 1951 there had been 519 children (infants and juniors) attending the Dollis Primary School there were now 592. In March 1952 the borough's education officer finally announced that the new Dollis Junior School, together with two other new county primary schools in the Borough of Hendon, would be ready for occupation immediately after the Easter holiday.

THE NEW SCHOOL

The new Dollis Junior School opened its doors as a separate school, with its own headteacher, on 29 April 1952, the first day of the summer term. Elsewhere in the borough two other new primary schools were also opened that day – Broadfields Junior School and The Fairway Junior and Infant School. The new Dollis Junior School was still not finished. The dining halls were not ready and the administration block was still under construction, which meant that during its first term the school's offices, staff rooms and store rooms had to be set up in the HORSA hut.

The school's first headteacher was Mr Harry Bryant, who had taught in Hendon schools for over twenty years, and had previously been the headteacher at Clitterhouse Junior and Infant School. Mr Bryant, the son of a Slough professional photographer, had started teaching in Buckinghamshire in 1922. Subsequently, in 1928, he took up his first position in Hendon at the Burnt Oak Council School, where his initiation to the Watling Estate schools had included the sight of some 2,000 people queuing for a place in the school, and the experience of teaching a class that was separated from its neighbour by nothing more than a curtain! From 1947 until his appointment to Dollis, he had been the headteacher at Clitterhouse. Mr Bryant's chief assistant (deputy headteacher) was C.N. Bissenden, 'a very experienced teacher' who had arrived in Hendon from Leeds only in January 1950. Bissenden had been responsible for the juniors in the old school, under its first headteacher, Miss A.M. Willis, but he soon left the new junior school to take up the headship of St Paul's Church of England School. Both he and Miss A. Nicholls, a veteran Hendon teacher who temporarily replaced him as chief assistant, were among those teachers who had first occupied the new junior school's classrooms. Mr Bissenden was ultimately replaced by Mr Cleaton.

The new Dollis Junior School was planned for a two-form entry, for boys and girls, aged seven to eleven, providing places for 320 children in all. There were seven regular classrooms and two larger general-purpose classrooms for such things as handicraft work. The spaciousness of the school's corridors, hall and entrance lobby made a good impression on visitors, and in addition to the necessary classrooms, it had 'administrative rooms, sanitary accommodation, a kitchen and dining room'. With these latter facilities – completely internal lavatories, a kitchen and a dining room – it was a very modern school. Many older Hendon schools had neither dining facilities nor internal lavatories – the latter not being finally improved in all local schools until the mid-1960s.

Despite the school's modern features, however, the Hendon Education Committee were not entirely happy. Whereas previously the committee itself had handled all aspects of such projects, as in the case of the original Dollis School, the planning and execution of the new Dollis Junior School (and Hendon's other new schools) had been done at county level. A few local feathers had clearly been ruffled as a result, and when in November 1954 HM Inspectors produced an 'adverse report' on the new Broadfields Junior School, supported by other observations as 'to the serious defects in the design and construction' of Hendon's other new schools, there was considerable anger. Committee members felt they had not been properly consulted over the building of the new schools, and they now wanted to insist that for the future, all new school buildings in Hendon be designed and constructed 'in Hendon'. In the end tempers cooled somewhat, and Middlesex County Council was simply urged to take 'action'.

At Dollis there were soon problems with the boiler house and fuel yard. In 1954 there was some expenditure on 'improvements', but the school's boiler troubles continued to simmer, and by June 1955 'urgent repairs' were called for, the Hendon Education Committee insisting that the remedial work be done according to the assessment of the borough's own surveyor and engineer, and *not* the county architect. The boiler dispute was only just cooling, when the temperature was again raised as a result of the school's first full inspection in November 1955. HM Inspectors might have been impressed by the spaciousness of the corridors, the hall and entrance lobby, but they were far less pleased, just as they had been the year before when they visited the new Broadfields School, with certain aspects of Dollis Junior's fabric and decoration. Although little over three years old, 'inferior paints' and poor ventilation (with attendant condensation) had left some of the walls 'much discoloured'. The inspectors were concerned that the building would lose its 'freshness and attractiveness' far sooner than had been planned for. In the classrooms themselves they found the artificial lighting to be poor, and the windows, apart from the French doors, to be difficult to open, which added to the ventilation problem.

As a result of HM Inspectors' report on Dollis Junior School, the redecoration of four Hendon schools, including Dollis, Broadfields and The Fairway, was ordered in March 1956 – the bill for Dollis was the highest, at £1,070. Problems with the decoration at some of the borough's new schools, however, did not go away. The finish on their internal walls proved impossible to clean without damaging the distemper itself. Only two years later the borough's education authorities were again looking at the need for further redecorating at Dollis, this time at a cost of nearly £2,000.

STILL MORE CHILDREN …

Awkward windows, poor ventilation, 'discoloured' walls and a cantankerous boiler were undoubtedly irksome, but of rather greater concern was the new headteacher's staffing problems. The school had started in 1952 with an experienced staff, all recruited from the original Dollis Junior and Infant school. A team spirit had been immediately apparent, and 'all were pulling together from the start', but 'promotion, marriage, removal and other factors' were soon to take their toll. By the time of the school's first inspection in November 1955, eleven out of a teaching staff of fourteen had been at Dollis Junior School only since August 1954, and two further changes were about to occur. HM Inspectors were understandably concerned about the effect that such an 'unsettled' staff was having on the children. Bryant's teaching staff had suffered more disruption 'than was normal or good for the school', but on the positive side the inspectors did note that many of the teachers were working 'steadily and well', though several had 'still to establish themselves'.

The inspectors were hopeful that the end of this unsettled period was at last in sight, but staffing problems were only one of Mr Bryant's worries. Indeed his staffing troubles were made worse by his other great concern: the ever increasing number of children coming to his school, as unremitting as it was unexpected. In little over three years the school had been 'filled to overflowing'. Bryant put the cause down to a change in Dollis's catchment area and to, 'an influx of large families in the Mill Hill East area'. The school had been planned for 320 places, and at its opening it had been predicted that the roll would, by January 1956, stand between 301 and 350 – but very soon the number of places was increased to 360 (by using both of the general-purpose rooms as classrooms, making nine classrooms in all, each intended for forty children). But the school's initial intake had been 332, and by January 1953 there were 370 on the roll. A year later there were 383, and by September 1955 the roll had climbed to 511, and the following January it was still 509.

When Dollis Junior School opened in April 1952 there were some 18,370 children in Hendon's schools, of whom roughly two thirds were in primary schools. The general school age population in Hendon had increased by 6.9 per cent between May 1952 and September 1955 – but at Dollis Junior School the increase had been 70.3 per cent, far outstripping any previous predictions. Mr Bryant's new school, though it had 'a spacious hall', wide corridors and a new dining room, had only nine classrooms. He clearly needed more accommodation for his children than that, and when HM Inspectors visited Dollis in November 1955 they found that Mr Bryant had in fact managed to find four extra rooms. One room he had found in the old school (now Dollis Infant School), another two had been found in the HORSA hut, and a fourth he had found by turning the teachers' staff room into a classroom. The dining hall was used for occasional lessons such as the girls' needlework classes – and also provided the venue for adult evening classes in dress making. Despite the large numbers of children, the inspectors felt there was, 'no impression of overcrowding because of the very generous provision of circulation space and the lack of need to regiment the children who have learnt to use the building well'. Apart from the rather large classes, the inspectors concluded that the working conditions within the school were, 'quite good' – what the children and their teachers (no staff room!) thought, is not recorded.

But the Dollis roll continued to climb, reaching 532 in the autumn of 1956, and was expected to be even higher the following year. Bryant admitted that the accommodation was being 'severely taxed' – he now had fourteen classes and fourteen teachers, which meant a temporary end to the instruction of the small remedial groups of 'backward children'. Even short illnesses among the staff caused considerable difficulties as no extra teacher was readily available. The worst of such times, however, was coming to an end. By September 1958 the tide of numbers began to recede, and the following year Bryant could note that the so-called 'bulge' had left the school. The estimate for the new term (autumn 1959) was only 374, and he felt able to end the junior school's use of classrooms in the infant school. Moreover, his staff had undergone fewer changes (resignations and necessary reductions just about balancing), and he was looking forward to 'working under more normal conditions', as the number of children in his school came closer to its original, planned accommodation.

In September 1960 the roll came down to 344 and dropped further during the year. Finally in September 1961, over nine years after the junior school had opened, the roll fell to only 325, bringing it to the level originally planned (320 places). As it seemed likely to remain at that level 'for some time', Mr Bryant at last felt able to use one of the general purpose rooms as originally intended. Hitherto the school had made use of the 'waiting space' outside the medical room as a library. Now, one of the general purpose rooms (room 9) became the school library and projection room (for 16mm films and film strips), and was also to be used for music and for radio broadcasts. Science and needlework lessons were to be given there as well, on recently acquired 'large tables'. Such a general-purpose room was considered to be of great importance to the school – it now relieved the assembly hall for physical education, apparatus work, drama, and country dancing.

Dollis at last settled down to a two-form entry school of eight classes, in two streams. In addition to which there were two smaller classes of less-able children, each class having a two-year age range. The first year children occupied the two classrooms in the HORSA hut; the others were taught in the main building. As well as the headteacher, there were ten assistant teachers. Mr Bryant reported 'a strong team spirit' among his staff. They were 'always ready to co-operate in any school activity'.

WHAT A DIFFERENCE A WAR MAKES!

The Hendon Education Committee made every effort to ensure that the original Dollis School of 1939 was built, decorated and equipped according to 'the best modern standards' and it was the committee's intention that its future extension would see 'another school of the same type and character' placed alongside it. This new school was to be 'almost a replica' – indeed one of the guiding factors in planning the original school was the creation of a scheme which would enable its future extension. Construction of the new junior school began only twelve years after work had first started on the old school, but the six years of war that had intervened had a decided impact on the outcome. Far from being 'almost a replica' of the pre-war school, its post-war sister could hardly have been more different.

Whereas in 1938, as a matter of civic pride, the Hendon Education Committee had sought only the finest building materials for a school which the mayor described as a 'notable addition' to the borough's educational stock, the Middlesex county planners of 1950 worked in an atmosphere dominated by the needs of post-war reconstruction and recovery. Labour and materials were in short supply. Housing was the national priority, but the Government was also committed to a greatly enlarged educational building programme, a result of the Butler Education Act of 1944. A report of 1948, made by the Government's technical working party on school construction, laid emphasis on economising. Educational projects were to be as economical as possible in their demands on labour, and every opportunity was to be taken to reduce 'the cubic content' of school buildings. Financial savings were to be paramount. Not only were the school planners of 1950 on the lookout for the cheapest materials, they were also ready to experiment with new ones in order to circumvent shortages in more traditional building supplies.

The Middlesex county architect was himself a member of the working party on school construction, and the new Dollis Junior School was built according to many of its recommendations, and subsequent Government instructions. The economising and experimentation of the post-war years, however, had some unforeseen consequences – certainly some of the new junior school's teething troubles were a result, and these in turn produced additional, and very unwelcome, costs. The builders of the new school were further hampered by inflation (particularly steep in the early 1950s), and by general shortages in building materials – some, at least, of the steel used for Dollis Junior was 'second hand material'. Where the pre-war Dollis had been built and equipped in twelve months for a cost of approximately £26,800, the post-war junior school took two years to complete, for a final bill of £111,621 15s 2d. The final cost of the new junior school was nearly 30 per cent more than the county council's original estimate of £86,080, and a further £1,070 had to be spent very soon after on redecoration, itself a result of trying to cut costs on materials. Various factors, not least inflation in the cost of both labour and materials, had resulted in the sharp difference in cost between the two schools – but there was more besides.

A TOUR OF TWO SCHOOLS

To any visitor in the mid-1950s the layout of the two Dollis schools presented an immediate and obvious difference between them. That difference, together with many other features, still reveals the very different circumstances in which the two schools were built.

Whereas both were of the 'bungalow type', neither of them being the two-storey, or even three-storey structures of earlier decades, the pre-war Dollis school was of a 'verandah' design, with an open loggia built around a quadrangle, while the post-war junior school was laid out in what the county architect described in November 1950 as, 'the conventional finger type school plan'. The classrooms of the pre-war Dollis stretched along the south side of its quadrangle with large windows and doors giving direct access to the playground, while on their other side they had folding screens opening into the loggia. It was designed with the intention of giving urban children a healthy dose of fresh air. The classrooms of the new junior school ran out as 'fingers' set at right angles to a main corridor, and were themselves placed on only one side of the smaller corridors so formed. Each classroom had windows and French doors opening into the playground, set on the wall opposite from that which formed part of the corridor. The 'finger' corridors themselves had ample windows, the finger plan being so designed for 'aspect reasons', i.e. to catch the day's sunlight. In the 'cold war' climate of the early 1950s it was considered that the classrooms of such schools could, if needed, be put to use as hospital wards.

The new Dollis Junior School was built in compliance with the Ministry of Education's 1949 'Amendment' of the Building Regulations for Schools, its general object being to reduce costs, while also allowing greater flexibility in planning, 'in order to leave scope for experiment, and to meet the needs of schools of unusual type or size'. The new instructions affected the internal layout of new schools, in particular changing the design and location of cloakrooms, lavatories and 'sanitary offices', and the provision of staff rooms. The requirements of the 1949 amendment affected Dollis directly, making many of its internal details different again from those of the older school.

Instead of actual cloakrooms, planners were encouraged to use part of the 'circulation space', placing such facilities along the corridors, either as shallow alcoves or by simply affixing the appropriate fittings to the corridor walls. Where the older Dollis had completely separate cloakrooms designated by age and sex, the new school had open bays set along the main corridor. The 1949 instructions both reduced the scale of provision for lavatories 'in the interest of economy', and also 'strongly recommended' that the wash basins of the hitherto separate 'lavatories' be put into the same rooms as the children's 'sanitary offices.' Where previously hot water had to be supplied to every wash basin, now it had only to be 'available' in every washroom. A new economising scale for the provision of sanitary offices was also introduced, drawn up according to, 'the probable peak use at certain times of the day'. Its principal target was junior boys. The new scale cut substantially the number of their offices, the planners being told that the number of WCs and urinals for these young scholars should now be assessed on a 'combined basis' – but always remembering that a certain proportion must be in the form of WCs! Happily the scale of provision for the girls was left largely unchanged. The new junior school conformed to the new rules, while also placing together its lavatories and sanitary offices in conjoined spaces. In the old school they remained separate, the boys' lavatory at some distance from their sanitary offices.

The new demands for compactness and economy spared neither children nor teachers. Previously such facilities as lavatories and cloakrooms for the adults (staff and visitors, such as the school doctor) had been provided in several parts of a school (as at the old Dollis), but now they were to be brought together as a single group in one location 'conveniently situated in relation to the Head's room, staff rooms and medical inspection room'. As a mixed-sex school of a certain size, Dollis Junior School was entitled to a separate room for its headteacher and, if the headteacher was a man, a further room for the school's senior mistress. Every school was to have a common room for its staff. This latter was duly provided for the new junior school but at the old school there had been two such staff rooms: one for the assistant masters and another for the assistant mistresses, with their own adjacent lavatories, and a kitchen adjoining that for the mistresses. For those first teachers at the new junior school who had known a more generous provision in the old school, a single common room must have seemed cramped – but worse was to follow. This sole refuge was soon pressed into service as an extra classroom. Whereas in the old school the staff rooms and other administrative rooms were incorporated well within a main building which included the classrooms and other facilities, in the new junior school they constituted an administration block, and were set along one side of a narrow corridor which was quite literally placed out on a limb, all but completely separated physically from the rest of the school. This arrangement was partly for reasons of economy in construction and partly to fit onto the land available. Indeed, the plans of other schools that were then being worked on by the county architect called for such administrative blocks to be simply 'connected' to the classroom blocks by a covered walkway.

The Government's Technical Working Party on School Construction, which reported in 1948, was following up on the work of a wartime predecessor established in 1943 to look into the standardisation and prefabrication of school buildings. In the event of a large-scale educational building programme being undertaken, it had been fully anticipated that there would have to be a wide use of prefabricated items, and that it would be unwise to tie such a programme to a regular and substantial supply of any one particular material. The materials would have to be inexpensive and easy to build with, saving on labour and allowing for quick construction. Innovation and experiment were thus greatly encouraged, with the working party looking at a range of new materials and construction methods for both permanent and 'demountable' school buildings. The working party considered cellular 'plastic' materials for walls, and compressed straw panels covered with bitumen felt (Stramit) for roofing. It examined various prefabricated reinforced concrete units, looking in one instance at wall and roof panels made of angle iron reinforced with chain link fencing and filled with concrete, intended to be simply bolted together.

This prevailing emphasis on both innovation and economy in the use of building materials resulted in further contrasts between the old and new schools. The original Dollis was brick built, its outer walls faced with 'hand made multi-coloured facing bricks', the inner walls of its quadrangle clad in white cement, and its pitched roofs covered with 'hand made sand faced tiles'. Internally its staff rooms and classrooms had floors made up of 'teak blocks laid on concrete'. The assembly hall had an attractive barrel ceiling with decorative details, its walls were panelled from floor to ceiling in oak and walnut, and its floor was done in oak strips. By comparison the builders of the new junior school made far greater use of prefabricated materials. As housing projects had the first claim on bricks, it was important to reduce their number. At the junior school much use was made of cement rendering (Mortone Render), in place of facing bricks, on the exterior walls. The outer walls of the finger corridors were of reduced height and the corridor roofs made flat, while the roofs over the classrooms themselves were pitched much lower than those of the old school – no waste of materials in pitching a higher roof over both corridors *and* classrooms. But fewer bricks could produce some pleasing results – along one side of the main corridor, glass blocks were used, an imaginative idea which both saved bricks and also let in more natural light.

Indeed, natural light was a feature that the county architect was keen to introduce wherever possible. With innovation and 'compactness' very much on the school planner's agenda, the county architect was designing other Middlesex schools which had classrooms on both sides of their corridors. It was a plan which, if it made for greater 'compactness', did so at the expense of natural light. Developing this plan further still, the county architect was designing a new type of two-storey school as well. In an attempt to counteract the loss of natural light in these designs a system of 'controllable top lights' was introduced. This new 'top lighting' consisted of long narrow windows, with shutters, running along the top of the classroom's corridor wall, set just above the corridor roof line (as the corridor roof was lower in height than that of the classrooms). In the words of the county architect, this new innovation allowed each teacher 'to control the intensity of light in each classroom at will' – the critical piece of equipment being a long pole (with hooked end) with which the shutters could be opened and closed from below. The new classrooms at Dollis Junior School, being built at the opportune moment, were duly given the county architect's new 'top lighting'.

Internally the new school was of very plain appearance compared to the older one. If its hall was large, it was also decidedly utilitarian – no elegantly curved ceiling and no wood panelling such as enhanced the appearance of the older school. The new junior school did, however, enjoy some advantages from its economising design: its new 'compactness' made it a better heated building. In the old school the tall classroom windows and doors, folding screens and open loggia were a pleasure in fine summer weather, but in winter there were cold draughts and many complaints. It was a circumstance that the new junior school was spared, but one that its older sister school had to endure, along with Hendon's other 'verandah schools,' until the 1960s.

WHAT'S IN A NAME?

Both the present-day Dollis Junior and Dollis Infant Schools trace their origin back to a single school: 'The Dollis Council Junior and Infant School'. However, when this school first opened on 1 May 1939, it did not use the name 'Dollis'. Throughout its planning and construction, the Hendon Education Committee had always referred to it as the 'Dole Street School' and when Miss Willis, its first headteacher, commenced her school log book to record daily occurrences she duly entered its name as the 'Dole Street Junior and Infant School'.

The 'Dole Street' name did not survive very long. By the time of the school's official opening by the Mayor of Hendon, hardly ten weeks later on 8 July 1939, the name had been changed to 'Dollis'. In the interim there had been a complaint from local parents over the use of the word 'Dole'. A letter had been sent to the council from a local resident pointing out, 'that the name savoured of an illusion to the benefit paid to the unemployed, which was rudely known as "the dole"'. In an era which had seen mass unemployment, when the Jarrow marchers had in November 1936 found overnight accommodation in Hendon schools, this was a sensitive issue, at least with some of the local parents.

On 23 May 1939, at their monthly meeting, the Hendon Education Committee debated the question of the school's name. 'Dole Street' itself was a name of considerable antiquity, a 'dole' being an apportionment of land. Changing its name clearly rankled with some of the committee members, but Councillor Hignett said that he had never thought 'Dole Street' a particularly 'high sounding name', and proposed 'Pursefield Manor School' instead. It was Major N.G. Brett-James, whose local historical knowledge was much respected, who brought the name of 'Dollis' forward, pointing out that it incorporated the 'Dole' name without any other associations – (indeed 'Dollis' may itself be a variant of 'Dole'). Noting the existence of both a Dollis stream and a Dollis farm (then recently pulled down), the Major proposed the name 'Dollis Farm School'. Councillor Hignett, who was still for a 'high sounding name', now suggested 'Dollis Manor School' – which the Major pointed out, was, like Hignett's earlier suggestion, entirely fictitious from an historical point of view. In the end the word 'Farm' was dropped (thank goodness!) and 'Dollis School' carried the day, eight votes to two.

THE DOLE STREET SITE

In the 1920s the area in which the future Dollis schools would be built was farmland. The actual site of the junior school was occupied by Elm Farm, a menagerie of farm buildings which lay on the western side of the now vanished 'Dole Street' (which ran from the corner of Wise Lane with Milespit Hill, down to Sanders Lane). The junior-school site was just north of a bridge (still extant, though much widened), under which ran the Finchley and Edgware line of the LNER (London & North Eastern Railway, first opened in 1867 as the Edgware, Highgate & London Railway). The rail line would eventually come to form part of the Dollis Junior School boundary (and in 1983, following the lifting of the tracks in 1967, a part of the track way would become the school nature reserve). Between the bridge and Elm Farm lay a smaller piece of land known as Canada Villa – a house built in 1898 by George Wooley and named in honour of his second wife who came from Canada.

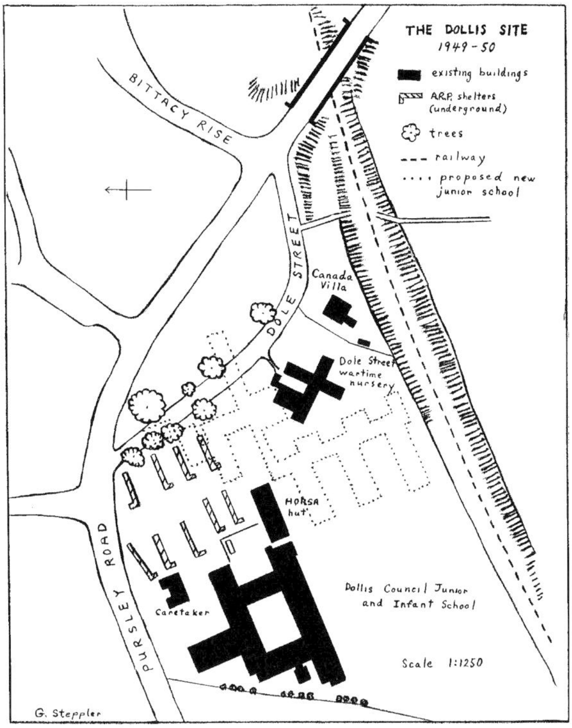
THE DOLLIS SITE
1949-50
existing buildings
A.R.P. shelters (underground)
trees
railway
proposed new junior school
BITTACY RISE
DOLE STREET
Canada Villa
Dole Street wartime nursery
HORSA hut
PURSLEY ROAD
Caretaker
Dollis Council Junior and Infant School
Scale 1:1250
G. Steppler

The Dollis site, 1949-50.

In 1930 Elm Farm was closed, and two years later its farmhouse was demolished. In 1935 Hendon Borough Council made a compulsory purchase of some 30 acres of farmland 'in the vicinity of Dole Street', on which to erect the new houses of its 'Dole Street Housing Scheme'. Some 5.44 acres were set aside for an elementary school and in 1938-39 the Dollis Council Junior and Infant School was erected on a plot to the north-west of the old Elm Farm.

As the construction of further housing in the area was fully expected, especially as there were then plans to electrify the whole of the LNER line to Edgware, it was intended from the beginning that a second school would be 'placed alongside' the first when the need arose. In design it was to have been 'almost a replica', built on the eastern side of the existing school, with a line passing through the centre of the caretaker's bungalow (still extant) forming, 'the central axial line of the completed group of buildings'. But the outbreak of war in 1939 changed everything. The land immediately to the east of the original Dollis School was used for the construction of the school's air-raid shelters (still extant) and when in the post-war years a new junior school was being planned, this posed a serious problem. The land to the east of the old school could no longer be used for the new extension, and it appeared that the new junior school would not only have to encroach on the existing school's playing fields and tar-paved area, but would itself be left with a very restricted access.

A solution was found in the plans to complete the construction of Pursley Road (begun in the mid-1930s), linking it with Sanders Lane. Completion of the new road would leave an area of land between the new road (now that part of Pursley Road running past the junior school) and that portion of Dole Street which ran to the east of the original Dollis Junior and Infant School. Acquisition of this land would add just over one acre to the school site, making up a total of 6.4 acres, of which half would be available for the new school. This would enable the new junior school to be planned with little loss to existing playing areas and would also allow much better access.

In the course of 1949 the new road was finished, and in September 1950 it was declared a 'public Highway.' In the meantime, in the spring of 1950, construction had begun on the classroom blocks of the new junior school, but nothing could be done on the remaining blocks until that portion of Dole Street which lay to the east of the old school had been 'stopped up'. This was dependent on obtaining an order from the Ministry of Transport, and not until the spring of 1951 was this part of Dole Street finally closed off, after which work began 'at once' on the remainder of the new school – its hall, administration block, kitchen, dining rooms and boiler house. In June of that year the new school buildings were described as being, 'on the site of the existing school, on the site of an old road rendered redundant by the construction of the new Sanders Lane and on the land situated between the old road and the new road'. The plans for the new school had to be adapted to the land available, but it is interesting to note that although laid out on a very different plan to that of the original Dollis, the new junior school classrooms were set on the same orientation as those of the old school, both using the same 'aspect' to catch the day's sunlight.

Elm Farm was long gone before the construction of the new junior school began, but during the war a 'wartime day nursery' (to enable mothers to do war work) had been established on the same site, just to the north of Canada Villa, its exact location having been partly on the site of the present school hall and its verandah, and stretching out onto the lower playground immediately south-east of the hall. Using pre-fabricated materials supplied by the Ministry of Health, work on the nursery had begun in July 1943, but it had not been ready for occupation until the following March, its completion delayed by difficulties in finding suitable labour to lay its drains. The nursery, complete with pram shed and brick-built air-raid shelter, had not been in use quite five months when, on the night of 3 August 1944, it suffered extensive blast damage to its roof and windows from a V-1 hit in the gardens of Bittacy Rise. The existing Dollis Junior and Infant School also suffered in the same blast. The damage had been quickly repaired and the nursery brought back into use, but in the course of constructing the new junior school the nursery had to be removed. At the same time Canada Villa, the other occupant of the area, was acquired by Middlesex County Council. This provided some additional land (with further small 'parcels' from the railway and from Hendon Golf Club) with which to complete the new school, and also allowed the whole of Dole Street to be closed up. In 1939 Canada Villa had been converted into a youth club but, much damaged in the 1944 V-1 blast, its post-war condition was never very good. From 1946 onwards there were various schemes proposed to improve it. Burglaries and vandalism took their toll too, and in 1958 the Mill Hill Youth Club was unable to use the premises, being forced instead to hire the hall of Dollis Junior School two evenings a week. Finally, in 1962, Canada Villa was demolished and replaced by the current building (of the same name), still retaining its function as a youth centre.

Today, if you stand on Milespit Hill and look towards the junior school, you can get a good idea of where the old Dole Street used to run. It ran straight ahead across the school grounds, to the right of the large tree, passing through the main school building in the area of the school office. It continued on towards the old Canada Villa (which was set further back than its current successor) and then swung left to meet the bridge over the railway. Set your imagination back 100 years; if you were standing where the school office is now you might have been in danger of being run over by a hay wagon heading down Dole Street – Hendon was famous for its hay!

School Life in the 1950s

GETTING TO SCHOOL

Travelling to school, like other activities, has its hazards, but would you include being bitten by a horse in Bunns Lane? One March morning in 1948 the headteacher arrived at school to discover that one of her young scholars had indeed been the victim of an unfortunate encounter with a horse! The child's mother being out at work, the headteacher had to take the child to the doctor's clinic herself. The junior children of 1950 walked to school on their own, either alone or with others. If you owned a bicycle you could ride but you would have to be careful of the traffic – four-wheeled, and four-footed! Because children travelled on their own, safety while making the journey to school was a matter of particular concern.

In the autumn of 1949, the Dollis headteacher, Miss Willis, was so concerned over the re-configuration of local roads (especially of Pursley and Milespit) then going on, that she herself (with four helpers), having first divided the whole of her young scholars into four groups according to where they lived, set aside an entire morning, 'to show each child where to walk and cross roads'. This she thought 'necessary to avoid accidents', and that November, Mrs Joyce, the road patrol for the new road, spoke to the juniors about the dangers of crossing the road to go to the new shops in Salcombe Gardens.

The Hendon Borough Council had its own regular Road Safety Campaign subcommittee which, in the summer of 1946, mounted a special Road Safety Exhibition at Hartley Hall, Mill Hill. Coinciding with this the police put on a Safety First on the Roads demonstration for the Dollis children. While teachers and children looked on, six officers, with cars, motorcycles and traffic lights (electrical) went through their paces on the school playground, the proceedings also coming under the gaze of the chief police commissioner, his assistant, and Hendon's education officers. For this big demonstration fifteen of the juniors brought their bicycles to put on their own cycling demonstration. Such displays by the police, with further visits by individual policemen to lecture on 'Safety First' were a regular occurrence.

Headteachers were urged to take every suitable opportunity to remind parents and children of the Road Safety Code and of the special rules for those who cycled to school. To further assist there were adult road-crossing patrols at points thought to be particularly dangerous – but the problem of who would provide these patrols, the police or local people, was a matter of long running contention; cuts and manpower shortages in the police were regularly blamed for any shortfall. At Dollis the police provided one such patrol for the railroad bridge on Dole Street (now part of Pursley Road), near Canada Villa, but in 1946, due to 'insufficient manpower', the police felt unable to continue their man there, and at other school crossings. A storm of protest from headteachers followed, with letters of objection even being sent to the Minister of Transport and to the Home Office. The final result, on this occasion, was the installation, in September 1946, of a local resident, Mrs Ivy May Maynard, as the first civilian road patrol for the Dole Street bridge. Following the opening of the new school in 1952, a separate road patrol was established for the juniors, removing some of the anxiety 'occasioned by the large number of children who had to cross and re-cross daily.' Pursley Road, however, was to remain a dangerous crossing spot for many years to come.

Because the children walked to school, they needed to be properly shod, and in the years of post-war austerity this meant keeping your shoes or boots (one pair only for many) in good repair. In the immediate aftermath of the war, the Hendon School authorities had even linked poor school attendance rates with the long periods of time which children had to wait to have their shoes and boots repaired – a result, they thought, of so many men who were normally employed as cobblers being still in the armed forces.

If, however, you lived far enough away from school, you might be entitled to free 'transport facilities' – free bus or train tickets, or a bicycle allowance – and in some cases a hired coach might be provided if an area was isolated and no public transport was available. Although the Borough of Hendon was quite generous, there were conditions to be met, and they give a good idea of the walking distances considered acceptable for children. Free bus tickets were issued to infant children with more than 1 mile to travel, and to juniors with more than 1½ miles to go. In 1950, however, as 'a measure of economy', Middlesex County Council changed the distances to 1½ and 2 miles respectively, and in 1952 adopted the even more demanding distances of the 1944 Education Act. Henceforth a child under the age of eight had to live at least 2 miles from school, and 3 miles if over that age, all measurements to be, 'by the shortest walking route'. Anything under those distances and you either paid for public transport yourself (if such was available), perhaps cycled, or most likely walked to school. The little victim of the horse bite was lucky in at least one respect, for in 1948 Miss Willis, the Dollis headteacher, owned her own 'motor' and was able to *drive* this unfortunate young scholar to the doctor.

THROUGH THE CLASSROOM DOOR

In the classrooms of the new junior school, the children sat in pairs. Their dual desks were of the locker type (with a lid). The new ones had separate chairs, the old ones had the seats permanently attached, and all were equipped with inkwells – which offered multiple possibilities for inky mishaps and mischief (plait dipping was a favourite). The desks were set out in rows across the room and, as overcrowding was soon a problem, even in this new school, they must often have been placed very close together.

The classrooms were relatively bare by comparison to the decorative displays of today (2007). When teachers needed a map for their lessons, they could choose from a number of roll maps in the school's possession, and in addition there were eleven maps from the Empire Marketing Board transferred to the new school in 1952, enough to hang one in each classroom. Many classrooms did have 'pets, nature tables with labelled specimens, and books of reference to assist identification'. These classroom displays were complemented by potted plants and tanks of tropical fish found in the entrance hall and main corridor. Indeed nature study seems to have been one of the school's strong interests, at least that was the impression that HM Inspectors had in 1955. For special occasions, such as the parents' open days, the children's work (especially handicrafts) were put on display and the classrooms were artistically decorated.

The school day for juniors had a morning and an afternoon session, the former from 9.00 a.m. to 12.00 p.m. and the latter from 1.30 p.m. to 4.00 p.m. There were two breaks, from 10.30 a.m.

to 10.50 a.m., and from 2.45 p.m. to 3.00 p.m. This was the regime established in April 1951, but previously the school day had started later at 9.30 a.m. and had finished at 4.30 p.m., with schools closing at 4.00 p.m. in the winter months. Over the lunch break you either ate a school dinner or you went home to get something from mother. If the day seemed long, there was always the possibility of a wave and whistle from a passing train – in 1952 there were no trees or bushes bordering the LNER track way and the trains were still running to Edgware.

Mr Bryant, as a headteacher, was rather more easy going than Miss Willis had been in the old school, and as a whole Mr Bryant's teaching staff were reported by HM Inspectors in 1955 to have, 'a very satisfactory attitude towards children', being, 'at pains to prepare their work and make it interesting'. But the rigor with which discipline was maintained in the classroom depended, of course, on the particular teacher. Certainly to older teachers, their pupils were 'scholars', a term which was a clear reminder of the serious purpose behind their young charges' presence in the classroom. Whether affable or otherwise, the instructions of all teachers were backed up by the sanctioning of corporal punishment. If a reprimand or a clip round the ears failed to make a sufficient impression, the cane stood ready to do its duty – children who were late three times could expect a caning across the hand. With some teachers, talking in class could put you at risk of being hit by thrown chalk or a blackboard rubber, or getting a sore palm from the smack of a wooden ruler. For those who did not know their lessons or were inattentive, there was the humiliation of being branded a dunce, together with the possible punishment of writing out innumerable lines in humble restitution. Children were generally well behaved in class, and if there were those teachers who were notable for shouting at children and throwing chalk, there were also others who managed without either. Nor should the stricter aspects of the classroom seem surprising when the juvenile courts handed out fines, even to junior-age children, for 'pedal cycle offences' (which included ignoring traffic signs, being without a light and carrying an extra person), for being found on an enclosed premises, for 'insulting behaviour' and for failing to attend school. Moreover, the Hendon Education Committee was in regular contact with the courts, and kept an eye on the statistical tally of juvenile offences.

Mr Bryant felt that the 'large majority' of Dollis children took their work 'very seriously', and in an age when homework was not assigned with the unremitting regularity it was later to acquire, he was happy to report that many were even, 'prepared to do some homework each week to augment their exercises in class'. Children were expected to work hard, learn their lessons and follow the rules – and could expect a reprimand or worse if they did not. But school was not all doom and gloom (really!). The early 1950s was also an era of youth clubs and summer camping. St Mary's church in Hendon, the A1 Dairies and RAF Hendon were all on the list of occasional local visits by Dollis children, and further afield there might be the rarer treat of a trip into London or to St Albans. There were visits to the Tower of London, the Natural History Museum and the London Planetarium. In 1953 the children visited College Farm in Finchley as part of a project on 'The breakfast table milk', and also made trips to the cinema to see the *Conquest of Everest*. That year too, a party of third-year children enjoyed a steamer trip on the Thames to see the docks and to study the river's shipping and commercial activities. There were also school camping trips (to Ivinghoe Beacon), and the annual sports days, one at your own school, and another at the Hendon inter-schools contest. At Christmas there were class parties and a school entertainment – perhaps a puppet show – and carol singing. And in 1953 there was a very special celebration: the Queen's Coronation. In addition to tea parties and concerts, the occasion was marked by giving each of Hendon's young scholars a booklet on the coronation ceremony. There were also souvenir mugs, the chance of an outing to the cinema to see the coronation film (a colour copy was purchased to show to Hendon school children) – and three days of extra holidays! During coronation week there was a Hendon Schools Pageant, to which

Dollis Junior School contributed a display of country dancing. With its spacious new hall, Dollis became the rehearsal centre for other schools. The school's own coronation celebration included an historical fancy-dress parade in the morning, followed in the afternoon by a film (using the school projector for the first time) and a picnic tea. Each child received, 'a boxed tea … suitable drinks and ice cream'. To make a permanent record of the occasion, ornamental trees were planted in the school grounds.

The Dollis children were described as 'lively and animated', approaching their work 'with eagerness'. The regional inspector, remarking unofficially, said that he found Mr Bryant's new junior school to have a, 'remarkably pleasant atmosphere resulting from the lively and friendly manner of many of the children'. Overall he and his fellow inspectors had a positive impression of both teachers and children. The school had every appearance of, 'a happy community in which the children were given every consideration and respond with great friendliness.'

WHAT SIZE IS YOUR CLASS?

Miss Neumann, 'complained of little voice yesterday so Mrs Milward took her class'. Large classes and crowded rooms took their toll on teachers. When Miss Neumann lost her voice in February 1948, the size of the junior classes at Dollis were larger than they had ever been. In January of that year the average class size was fifty-three, with three of the junior classes having fifty-four children in them. Classroom teachers faced these numbers on their own. There were no classroom assistants, though the headteacher, Miss Willis, always tried to have one or even two 'floating teachers' who could step in when a colleague went ill (which seems to have been a frequent occurrence), but otherwise, as often as not, they ended up helping the headteacher herself with the endless drudgery of 'clerical work.'

The development plans of the local education committee came and went, being often amended as the forecast for the school age population fluctuated. There was great concern to reduce the crowding and to quite literally find everyone a chair to sit on! Providing adequate accommodation was a pressing necessity, but there was also a desire to improve the teacher/pupil ratio. During the war an ideal ratio of about one teacher to thirty pupils had been talked about, but the existing reality in 1943, in Hendon primary schools, was then an average of one teacher to forty-eight children. In the years immediately after the war the situation showed no improvement. At Dollis it became even worse, prompting a succession of class reorganisations in an attempt to improve things. At the start of the autumn term in 1951 the average Dollis junior class had forty-six children, but one class had forty-eight.

There was much hope that the new junior school would relieve the situation, but new headteacher Mr Bryant was almost immediately faced with rapidly growing numbers, which soon overtook the school's intended capacity of 320 children. By the autumn term of 1955 the school roll stood at 511, which would have meant an average of more then fifty-six children in each of the school's nine classrooms. But, as we have seen, Mr Bryant had managed to find four extra rooms for his children which allowed him to create thirteen classes, giving a much better average of just over thirty-nine children per class. This was certainly an improvement on the situation in the old school but still far from the ideal ratio discussed during the war years.

There was, however, a silver lining of sorts to this dark cloud, for the nadir of the overcrowding problem had finally been reached. Subsequently the numbers on the Dollis Junior School roll receded: there were 413 in May 1959, but only 366 that same autumn, and a decline continued thereafter. Sensing a brighter future, the Government's new School Regulations of 1959 set out a ratio for primary schools of one teacher to forty pupils, which it hoped would not be exceeded, except in 'unavoidable circumstances'. From 1962 onwards an improvement in the teacher/pupil ratio was discernable in schools throughout England and Wales. At Dollis the roll in September 1962 was down to only 322.

It was hoped that as resources permitted, the teacher/pupil ratio would be 'progressively' improved upon by local authorities, 'to bring the standard of staffing in primary schools closer to that in the lower forms of secondary schools'. The school age population, however, is always subject to fluctuations. In the late 1960s the number of primary school children was again 'steadily increasing'. At some schools there were serious difficulties. By the end of the decade, the Dollis roll was up to 400, much inflated by the addition of children from Inglis Barracks. Accommodation had to be found and at Dollis, as elsewhere, the answer was the 'mobile' and the 'demountable' classroom – or just plain 'hut'. Despite this situation, it was still hoped to improve the teacher/ pupil ratio, and in 1969 there appeared new regulations on the staffing of schools. The following year the Borough of Barnet decided, 'as a first step', to limit the size of its primary school classes, whenever possible, to thirty-five pupils and 'to regard a school as full when the average size of classes in the school reached that figure'. That autumn (1970), however, the third-year classes (fifth year in current parlance) at Dollis Junior still had forty-three children each. A year later the situation had improved – there were no classes of forty or over, but eight classes were still in the thirty-five to forty range.

Thanks to a declining birth rate the new goal proved attainable, and the concern over finding adequate accommodation experienced in 1969, had become by 1977 one of worry over 'falling numbers and school closures'. In the summer of 1979, at the end of Mr D.A. Heasman's first year as headteacher at Dollis, the roll had declined to 327. Dollis class photographs of the year 1981/82 reflected the then current trend in primary school numbers. The average across the twelve classes was less than twenty-four pupils per class, but in the top year it was over twenty-seven, while among those just starting in junior school it was less than twenty-two. And in 1950 Miss Willis thought thirty was 'a small class'!

Making an accurate forecast is strewn with many pitfalls including the completely unpredictable (such as a sudden surge in immigration). In the late 1970s it was predicted that there would be a substantial fall in the 1980s of the number of both primary and secondary school children, but that the numbers would again increase in the 1990s. And so it was that in 1978, prompted by a request from the Barnet Teachers' Association, the local education committee adopted a new teacher/pupil ratio, which it hoped would not normally be exceeded, of one teacher to thirty children. It was of course the ideal ratio talked of in 1943, and it has remained a quasi-standard against which class size is popularly measured.

In the 1990s numbers did rise again – as predicted! At Dollis the number of children rose steadily (as did the school's popularity and reputation), from 360 in 1993 to 472 by the end of the decade. In the process three new permanent classrooms were added and the number of classes increased from twelve to sixteen, making a four-form entry. By January 2002 the number on the roll had reached 505; a year later it was 513. On the way the school's average teacher/pupil ratio inevitably changed, from 27.6 in 1995 to 30.3 by January 2001, reaching 32.1 in 2003, with the largest class having thirty-four pupils.

TEACHING AND LEARNING: THE THREE Rs

Apart from Mr Bryant, the headteacher, there were fourteen teachers at Dollis Junior School in 1955. Thirteen were class teachers, and a fourteenth, a 'floating teacher,' was used to make up smaller groups for needlework and handwork – the boys generally worked at the latter in half classes. In the upper school (years three and four) there were two classes in each year, with a further 'remove class' for 'the more backward children'. The lower classes, years one and two, had four classes each. As was normal practice, the classes were streamed, and within each class each child was assigned their class position on the basis of regular term tests. In years one and two, however, Mr Bryant had established, 'parallel A classes and parallel B classes on a half yearly age basis', an unusual arrangement which the inspectors thought had much to commend it, as it sought to avoid some of the evils of a straight grading of the children from A to D.

The 'schemes of work' which headteachers prepared in 1950 to guide the assistants (the masters and mistresses) under their direction were intended to lay a sound foundation in 'the three Rs' – reading, writing and arithmetic. The term tests which Dollis junior children wrote gave a clear indication of where the academic emphasis was placed. There were eight papers, worth a total of 485 marks: composition 50, English 50, writing (i.e. handwriting) 25, dictation 50, reading 50, arithmetic 100, mental arithmetic 60 and general knowledge (also called general intelligence) 100.

Teaching literacy was fundamental, and the inspectors were particularly pleased with the reading work being done at Dollis. They noted with approval that at every stage the more backward children were taken out of class and given special tuition. The inspectors felt certain that this would ensure that all of the children who passed through the school would leave it being able to read.

The young Dollis scholars read their way through the school's stock of junior reading books: the *Laurel and Gold* series, and other junior 'readers' such as *The Adventures of Reading* and *Joy Rides in Bookland*. Books were loaned to Dollis, as they were to other Hendon schools, through the borough's public library service, and by supplementing the school's own books, this enabled Dollis to have a reading stock 'of attractive story books and the beginnings of a suitable reference library'. When the school first opened, the books were kept in cupboards which stood in a corridor recess, but by the autumn of 1955 they were described as being mostly distributed among the classrooms. This situation, the inspectors observed, did not cater for the school's best readers as all children seem to have been confined to selecting only books from their own classroom. The school did possess a further reserve of supplementary readers, specifically for the more advanced of its young scholars: among them were the classic adventure stories of *King Arthur and His Knights, Robin Hood, Ivanhoe* and *Swiss Family Robinson*.

There were literature lessons and verse-speaking lessons. Children stood up and read aloud to the whole class. The junior school possessed eighty-two copies of Oxford University Press's *Handbook of Speech Training*, and with further help from Schofield's *Speaking and Acting* series, the children both wrote and produced their own plays and presentations. In the top class (form VI), 'lecturettes and dramatization' were especially popular, allowing greater scope for imagination and creative initiative than was offered elsewhere in the school curriculum. Poetry was also on the junior curriculum, and in 1955 it seems to have been undergoing a bit of a revival at Dollis, after a period of relative neglect. The school possessed a number of different texts, from the no doubt precisely titled *One Hundred Poems for Children*, to the rather more intriguingly named *Stardust and Silver*. Poetry was to serve both as 'a source of language' and as an opportunity for clear speaking and expression. This, and drama work, were intended to give the children 'confidence and poise'.

Text book series such as *Common Sense English, Objective English* and *Introduction to the King's English*, though they might not evoke much curiosity through their titles, did lay the foundations of English grammar. And if there were still some unsteady scholars after the class had been put through the *Train and Test* series, they might yet be saved by the aptly named *First Aid in English*. The *Spell Well Word Books* hopefully helped young scholars to do just that, and as a further help in grasping the language, it was intended that each child have a copy of the Collins *Junior Dictionary*.

Proper diction and correct grammar were deemed an important part of the education of each child and although the inspectors who visited the juniors in the old school in 1950 were satisfied with this aspect of the school's work, they did feel that opportunities for original creative writing were not used as much as they could have been. Notwithstanding, some classes did produce a wall 'news sheet', and in Mr Kitson's class the children were also in regular correspondence with a school in Birmingham. In 1955, by way of contrast, HM Inspectors were pleased to find Mr Bryant's children writing 'so frequently about their interest in other subjects', though they did remark that in some classes a 'more disciplined writing based upon careful oral preparation' was needed if the quality of expression was to improve.

The study of arithmetic included both written and oral work. The texts included *Larcombe's Junior Arithmetic*, *Constructive Arithmetic* and Nesbit's *Supplementary Exercises* to which the school added ten sets of Pitman's *Accuracy Arithmetic* cards. In their lessons the children did mechanical sums and problems, while good teaching in arithmetic was also held to include 'much oral work and many number games'. The inspectors of 1955 did think that the teaching of arithmetic would be better if practical problems were used more often as a starting point for lessons, and as a basis for, 'a sound understanding of units and common relationships'. Nonetheless, there was 'careful work' to be seen at each stage, though the inspectors did lament the often slow progress made in the children's mathematical table work – a concern which seems to have a long and continuing history!

General intelligence was included in the formal term tests, and had its own special text books. *The Kingsway Intelligence Test – Pupils Edition* was unmistakably one; another was the more provocatively titled *Work This Out*. History, geography and nature study were also taught, and although they were not included in the formal term tests, they could be examined at the discretion of individual teachers, and would in either case be included in each young scholar's report. History and Geography touched on both Britain and other lands, and included a look at the local community. The teachers' reference library at Dollis included books on both Mill Hill and Hendon, though the school lacked suitable local maps of a large scale. The main emphasis in history lessons was on 'how people lived in earlier times', with drawing and modelling being 'freely used by way of record' in most classes. Some 'quite useful books' were available to support such work, but the inspectors did offer some advice, that 'it should be remembered that the children will be made to think more by translating a verbal account into pictures or pictures into words, rather than by copying either'. Nor were teachers to overlook the importance of 'testing and revision' in these subjects!

The nature study lessons, given once a week to each of the junior classes by Miss Williams, were particularly praised by the inspectors who visited the old school in May 1950. Miss Williams was an experienced teacher 'of considerable ability' who, amongst other things, specialised in nature studies, and the inspectors found her work 'outstandingly good'. Like all the best teachers, her enthusiasm, knowledge and 'the freshness of her treatment' had produced excellent results. Through 'nature tables, attractive reference books, class and individual nature note books, the planting of seeds and the good use of neighbouring ponds', she 'inspired children to find and do things for themselves'. It appears that when the inspectors next came to Dollis, to the new school in 1955, the passion for nature had quite literally grown and spread, so much so that it was noted that the school was giving 'considerable attention' to it, a fact which the displays of plants and tropical fish in the entrance hall and corridors made immediately obvious. Moreover it was a theme repeated through the pets and nature tables (with labelled specimens) found in many classrooms. The inspectors thought the displays created a good environment for such study, but wondered if more could be done with the material available, in training the children to be careful observers, and in giving incidental lessons rather than always waiting for the next set nature lesson. Miss Williams had come to the old Dollis School in September 1949 and at first had been a 'floating' teacher. She must have made an immediate impression on the school and subsequently was established with her own class of juniors in one of the prefabricated HORSA classrooms.

'USEFUL WORK': PURSUING OTHER ACTIVITIES

The school day began with 'a simple act of communal worship', which the inspectors of 1955 thought set 'a suitable keynote for the school day'. Religious instruction was largely in the form of Bible stories, related to the children 'in simple language and with sincerity'. In some classes, like Mr Kitson's, these scripture lessons were opportunities to dramatise the events, and as the school had a good supply of biblical pictures, these were also used in telling the stores. Although the stories tended to be told in isolation from each other, which could leave children uncertain as to the full sequence of events, many of the young scholars were reported to be inspired, 'writing to the full limit of their command of language in notebooks and folders'.

Painting and drawing were used for 'expression work of all kinds', being done both to tie in with other subjects (such as history and geography) and also to simply 'stimulate imagination and evoke a pleasing response from the children'. Music, too, was something the children enjoyed greatly. Hymns were a regular feature at assemblies, with each child in possession of a copy of the *School Hymn Book*. For their music lessons (which were twice a week in the old school), the classes were often grouped together in order that they could be taught by those teachers (there were four in 1955) who had musical ability. The lessons consisted mainly of singing and 'the rudiments of theory learnt through listening'. The school had a choir, and in 1955 there was a small recorder group that met after school. As the classes were frequently grouped together, the large number of children tended to make for singing that was more noted 'for vigour than sensitivity'. They sang 'heartily and tunefully', and if good phrasing was often lacking, the children did get an unmistakable enjoyment out of the musical experiences they were offered. Beyond the formal instruction of the classroom, thanks to the willingness of teachers to give up some of their own time, there was a drama group and country dancing.

Lessons in road safety (Safety First) were also a regular occurrence – a necessity as so many children made their way to school on their own – and included talks and demonstrations by the local police. On at least one occasion the constables even brought a lorry, a motorcycle, and their own 'road' and 'pavement' to Dollis. But the regular school lessons themselves also had a practical side. While the junior boys did handwork, the girls did needlework. Mr Bryant was credited with making 'a generous provision for a number of crafts', and the junior boys did weaving and basketry with cane and raffia, bookcraft (bookbinding), fretwork, and clay and paper-model making. The girls, under the charge of the school's needlework mistress, made a variety of items while being instructed in a number of processes. The older girls made a notebook record of what they learned, and their handiwork was carefully graded by the mistress, being subsequently offered for sale to parents. In the old school, while the junior girls had been under Miss Willis, herself an able seamstress, their efforts had been put to immediate practical use as the best girls were set to work in her own office making dusters and embroidering 'Dollis' on the school towels and nursery overalls. Mr Bryant's office did not bear witness to such industry – in the new junior school it was the dining hall, well light by its large windows, that was the venue for the girls' needlework sessions. The inspectors of 1955 acknowledged the good work being done at the school though they were not so impressed by the older boys! They urged the teachers to be more 'adventurous' in their craft projects.

When all is said and done, work alone, without physical exercise, can make anyone a dull scholar. The school had a football team for the boys and a netball team for the girls, while PT (physical training) lessons offered a chance for everyone to blow out the cobwebs and let off pent-up energy. In their physical education lessons the children did 'useful work', performing on the agility apparatus in the hall, while outdoors they made keen use of the school's small games equipment. There was football, netball, rounders, skittles, ten quoits, cricket and stool ball – and there was also a weighed rope for tug-of-war. But PT also included the gentler pursuits of swimming and dancing. A coach took children to the Mill Hill pool for swimming lessons, while back in school both girls and boys had regular dancing lessons, learning the steps and twirls of popular folk dances, English and foreign. All this activity was hard on footwear, and to keep young feet active the school maintained a 'consumable' stock of plimsolls, which were regularly 'redistributed'. They were kept in cages in the hall, the old pairs being put to salvage when the headteacher declared them to have finally become too unsightly, or too pungent (!) for further use.

DINNER TIME!

School dinners are often well remembered by those who ate them! In 1950 the arrival each morning at Dollis Junior and Infant School, of the van from the School Meals Service heralded the approach of the dinner hour – and hopefully the deposited containers would not have to stand for too long before their contents were dished out to the waiting diners! Tables were set out in the school hall and the places set by some of the older girls. It was not convenient that the hall was also being used as a classroom but in many other schools there was even less space, and children ate regularly in certain of the classrooms. The opening of the new junior school brought with it a school kitchen and dining halls to serve both infant and junior children. Such amenities were 'very much appreciated'. Having dinners cooked on the premises and served direct to the tables gave both schools a service 'of very high standard' and, Bryant noted, all of his staff stayed for the midday meal, both teachers and children eating together in the dining hall.

The School Meals Service had begun in Hendon in 1922, with twenty-four children being served a noon-time meal at a cost to the borough of 8d a head. By 1950 over 40,000 meals were being served each week, delivered to the Hendon schools from several central school kitchens (Dollis dinners came from Abbots Road) by a small fleet of vans – in 1954 there were five. The borough was intent on improving its service, and in 1948 a long-term plan had been drawn up for providing as many schools as possible with better dining areas and their own kitchens, or at least sculleries. The aim was to be able to serve meals to 75 per cent of the Hendon school population. The Dollis School was included in the scheme, the intention being to build on the 'school playing field' a 'combined kitchen and dining room' to serve 500 meals. Shortly thereafter, when the new junior school was finally built, it included a proper kitchen and dining rooms for both infants and juniors.

If, in 1950, the mention of school dinners did not always go down well with children, nor did it with teachers, not least with the headteacher. The problem was the amount of clerical work which school meals entailed, added to which was the matter of supervising the young diners! In 1950 headteachers were expected to be involved in both. Hendon headteachers had been very displeased at the county's decision in 1949 to abolish the post of dining-hall supervisor at each school, shifting the responsibility instead onto the senior server (whose salary was less than that of a supervisor) and the headteacher, 'who would be required to take over responsibility for the clerical side of the work'. Mrs Jaques, who was Miss Willis's secretary (but only part-time), had her time at school 'almost wholly used in the clerical work of the school meal' which meant that the school's other administrative work was done by the headteacher herself, with the help of other teachers. If Mrs Jaques was absent, it fell to Miss Willis herself to see that the 'dinner returns' were done. In addition Miss Willis might also do a turn at dinner-time supervision.

In 1951 the matter of school dinners seemed to be causing everyone indigestion. The National Association of Headteachers discussed it at a conference, where concern was expressed for the very fabric of school life, such was the general waste of staff time on school meals. Of particular annoyance was the disruption caused by the collection of the dinner money. Indeed this was what annoyed Miss Willis the most, for it meant her having to make a weekly trip to the bank with a sack full of coins. The weekly takings usually amounted to about £20 (but one week it was £27), almost entirely in copper and silver, and it was 'very very heavy to carry'. It was much too heavy for poor Mrs Jaques to carry on foot, for unlike the late dinner supervisor, she had no bicycle, all of which meant that Miss Willis had to use her own 'motor' and her own petrol – facts which she made very clear to the local education officer!

Nor were school dinners the only bone of culinary contention being discussed in Hendon's council chamber in the early 1950s: extra spoons and milk bottles were also on the menu! In January 1950 the councillors were informed that the Ministry of Education would allow school children an extra fork, in addition to the authorised allowance of one knife, one fork and one spoon. Rather innocently, as it turned out, the Hendon councillors thought it would be beneficial if they could also obtain permission for the younger children to be equipped with an extra spoon as well – for there was a stock of 600 teaspoons that had been in Hendon's possession 'for a number of years'. Middlesex County Council was urged to approach the Ministry of Education on Hendon's behalf, but the ministry refused the request, apparently without giving any reason. Quite dissatisfied, the councillors directed the town clerk to approach the local MP Sir Hugh Lucas Tooth (perhaps not inappropriately named in view of his mission), to see if he could elicit an explanation concerning the spoons from the Minister of Education himself. But a year after it had begun, the councillors were still puzzling over their failure to secure the release of their own teaspoons, and by then they were also involved in a tussle with Middlesex County Council over the handling of school milk which, until 1971, local authorities were obliged to provide. The Hendon councillors wanted to involve the 'school keepers' (caretakers) in its distribution, wished to appoint 'milk assistants' and also wanted 'senior pupils' to be allowed to carry the milk crates. The Hendon councillors also thought that it would be nice if in future the roundsmen were required to deliver their milk straight to each classroom door – now that would have been service! The Middlesex County Council, however, being rather more interested in the possibility of spilt milk and broken glass (and who would be held responsible for it) said 'no', stressing that both pupils and teachers were 'in no circumstances' to carry milk crates! This of course did not help schools to distribute the daily milk ration – and two-and-a-half years after it was first raised, the riddle of the milk crates and who could carry them, remained unresolved.

The point of all this effort was a scrumptious school dinner – an effort made all the more demanding, as until 1954 school meals were provided all year round, including school holidays. HM Inspectors looking at Hendon schools in the 1950s, though they did pass most dinners as at least 'satisfactory', were clearly not impressed by the culinary endeavours of every school kitchen. At the worst one, the dinners were, 'far from satisfactory. In particular the potatoes and second courses were badly cooked and unpalatable …' More commonly the criticism was that the portions, especially of meat, were too small, that meals were not hot enough, that drinking water was not available and that menus might be more imaginative. Good meals might be improved nutritionally by, 'an increased amount of fresh and dried milk and of fat.'

The kitchen at Dollis Junior School seems to have opened for business on 10 April 1952, serving meals during the Easter holiday, just prior to the formal opening of the school at the end of that month. The dining halls, however, were not ready until the autumn, 'early in the

Christmas Term'. When inspectors visited the school kitchen in 1955 they found the dinners to be 'well cooked and adequate', the service 'brisk and orderly'. They also noted that there was 'little waste', a remark they did not make of other schools, yet one which ties in closely with the recollection of former Dollis pupils. The school does seem to have run a strict policy of 'waste not, want not'. Alison Wray (1967-1971) thought the dinner ladies, 'must have had strict instruction not to let us duck out of getting some of everything on our plate. And once on the plate we had to eat it.' Although she thought the meals overall were 'excellent' (save for the soggy chips!), the cauliflower cheese made her 'feel sick' – but she needed both a note from home and an accompanying teacher to stop the redoubtable dinner ladies from giving her a helping! *All* of the food served out was meant to be eaten, and those young diners who failed to do so within the allotted time, were ordered to the dining-hall windows where they were expected to complete the task. The dining-hall window ledge was host to Dollis' tardy diners for many years, from the 1950s through the 1960s and 1970s. In warm weather, when the windows were conveniently left open, unwanted portions had a habit of disappearing very suddenly!

The austerity of the post-war years lingered on well into the 1950s, and its memory beyond that. If Dollis seemed hard on children who did not eat all they were given, one might spare a thought for one very unfortunate employee of the School Meals Service itself, who in 1957 was arrested and brought to trial for taking 'some meat, pieces of tart and a bottle of milk' from a school kitchen. It was accepted by the court that all of the items removed would in any case have been thrown out, and that the accused had taken them only in order to feed his family, having not yet received his first wages from the council. He was nonetheless fined £2 10s, though it cannot be imagined from the evidence presented how he could have been expected to pay this within the time allowed. Any leniency in view of the circumstances of the case was confined to allowing the accused to at least keep his job. The Dollis attitude to 'wasteful' children need not seem very surprising.

Whatever the personal memories of school meals might be, in the 1950s the demand for school dinners exceeded the means to supply them and the facilities to eat them in. At Dollis Junior School the proportion of children having school meals rose from 56 per cent in the autumn of 1956 to over 77 per cent by the autumn of 1961. Three years later it was over 80 per cent, and in the autumn of 1966 was reported to be nearly 94 per cent. Bryant attributed the rise partly to social changes in the area, but also to the excellence of the dining facilities at his new school. It was a situation which did not survive the inflation of the late 1960s and early 1970s, when headteachers and local school authorities had to face a new 'problem' – the rise of the sandwich eater! At Dollis their numbers rose from 14 per cent in 1972 to 20 per cent by 1976. Two years later nearly a quarter of the school's children were consuming sandwiches. For as the cost of school dinners rose, the number of sandwich-eating children increased too – and these were children who not only reduced the dinner-money takings, but also made a mess (that someone would have to clear up). They demanded a place to consume their crusts, and even required extra supervision! Some headteachers refused to allow them drinks (even their own drinks!), while others would not allow sandwich eating on school premises, or simply tried to ban it altogether. Recruiting enough mealtime supervisors was already a problem, and it was suggested that the sandwich eaters should pay a charge to cover their own supervision. The Secretary of State for Education and Science sent out a circular in February 1971, advising local authorities to make all reasonable provision for school sandwich eaters, to include tables, chairs, glass-ware and … cutlery (for cutting sandwiches?). That October, Hendon headteachers agreed that their sandwich eaters should be allowed to bring their own drinks to school but much was still to be left to the discretion of each headteacher. Only grudgingly were the sandwich eaters given a space – not always the most comfortable one!

THE SCHOOL YEAR

The outline of the school year in the 1950s was pretty much as it is today. The autumn term began in the first days of September, there was a Christmas holiday, followed by a spring term and another holiday at Easter, before the final, summer term. About the third week in July the school closed for a summer vacation. There was a half-term week about the end of October, another in February, and a final one, usually mid to late May, for Whitsuntide.

Early September saw the teachers and their scholars settling in. For the headteacher it was a time for handing out 'stock' (and carefully recording the same), for sorting out both the library books and the time tables, and for any number of other 'clerical tasks' – not least the preparation of the next 're-distribution' of plimsolls! For the young scholars the autumn half-term break was followed all too soon at the end of November by the year's first term tests – a number of which were set by the headteacher, who was always involved in scrutinising, if not marking, the papers. The ordeal lasted for a week but its finish brought you into December and its ultimate promise of Christmas! There was admittedly still the little matter of the reports which went home to mother and father (following the term tests), but once that was out of the way there was a 'Christmas Entertainment' to be enjoyed, usually about the middle of December. Puppet shows were especially popular ('The Mercury Marionettes' made a big hit at Dollis in the late 1940s). In 1951 there was an extremely good Punch and Judy show, while the year before a musician, Mr Whitely, had been 'much enjoyed by the whole school'. There might also be a nativity play by the children, and there were always individual class parties. Parents were also invited to an 'open' afternoon on which they could visit the school. On the last day of the term, at the closing assembly, there was carol singing.

School reopened in early January, and by the middle of February those who were in their final year at Dollis would be sitting another set of exams, this time the entrance examinations for secondary grammar school. Dollis was closed for 'ordinary purposes' for two days while these children wrote, their teachers supervised, marked the papers and made out the returns, and finally the caretaker took the whole lot to the Education Office in Hendon. The final results would not be known until June. The number of grammar-school places which the Dollis children secured would be carefully counted, for, as Mr Bryant observed in 1959, it 'has been some measure of the success of the quality of the teaching and of the standard attained in the classrooms'. In its first year the new junior school sent thirty-five children on to secondary grammar schools, but over the next three years there were only sixty-seven more successes, a decline which coincided with the relentless rise in the number of children attending the school, coupled with a high turnover of staff. But as both the staff and the number of children settled down, the rate of success improved. In two years, over the 1957-59 academic years, Mr Bryant was pleased to note that seventy-three children managed to secure grammar-school places. Setting up the entrance examinations involved a considerable amount of 'clerical work' on the one hand, and revision on the other, and the Easter vacation, when it finally arrived, probably seemed none too soon.

The first day of May, while Miss Willis was headteacher of both juniors and infants, was always special. On that day, or as close to it as possible, she celebrated the school's birthday (the birthday of the original Dollis Junior and Infant School, 1 May 1939), with a service in the hall – hymns, prayers, and a talk on the school – followed by a half hour of play to round off the celebrations! When possible, Empire Day (24 May) was also marked although sometimes the school was closed at this time for the Whitsun recess. A special service was again held in the school hall which, in 1951, featured prominently the playing of gramophone records of a patriotic nature, the singing of the national anthem and the saluting of the flag (as it was draped over the platform table). Memory of the all too recent war and the current tension in East-West relations must have added an extra edge to that year's commemoration. There were lessons on the Empire and a special broadcast for schools – and the afternoon, as was usual for this occasion, was granted as a holiday.

May was also the time of year when plans were being made for the annual sports days – one at Dollis and another inter-school sports at the Burroughs playing field in Hendon. Under Miss Willis, captains and vice-captains (of boys and of girls) were given their badges of office, and the school houses (named after the four national patron saints of the British Isles) got ready for the coming competitions. Just prior to the Dollis sports day, heats were run off in preparation for the races on the big day. Parents came in large numbers to watch, and some were invited to act as judges and starters. As with many school occasions, local councillors were often present, and could be called upon to make both presentations and speeches! A shield was presented to the winning house, cups to the champion girl and the champion boy, and fountain pens to the runners-up. Afterwards the staff, judges and local notables enjoyed tea and cakes in the staff room. For the inter-school sports, the children went to Hendon and the school was closed for the day.

The timing of the Dollis sports day (held in June or early July) varied from year to year. In 1950, however, Miss Willis decided that sports meetings were not practical that year, 'owing to a restricted playing field and building operations' (the new school). The following year Dollis children were again out of luck as the school's own sports day was cancelled the very day after the arrangements for it had been made. The headteacher arrived at school to find the playing field being ploughed up – no one had thought to tell her, and the education officer thought it had already been ploughed the previous autumn! Instead of a sports day, the children were told to keep off the freshly seeded playing field.

Mr Bryant's new junior school soon followed suit in establishing its own annual sports day, an event which continued to be extremely popular. There was, 'a full programme of running, jumping and team games contested on a House basis' while, 'a display of country dancing adds colour and music to the afternoon's activities'. Mr Bryant noted with satisfaction that over 90 per cent of the children took some active part in sports day. Moreover, the new junior school soon made its mark in inter-schools sport. The 1958/59 season was especially noteworthy. The football team won the Douglas Martin Cup for the second consecutive year, the school's swimming team took first place in the Primary Schools Swimming Gala, the girls' relay team won the cup at the Hendon Schools Athletics meeting and the boys won the final of the junior schools cricket competition, after what Mr Bryant described as 'a most exciting match'.

Spring and early summer also became the time for something very special – for Dollis junior children in their final year it became the occasion for the annual 'school journey'. The school's first such venture took a party of forty-two fourth-year children to the West Country in the summer of 1957. A 'complete success' ensured its repetition with double parties over the next two years, and it soon became a tradition for fourth-year (final) pupils. Transport was by a private coach which remained with the party for an eight-day excursion which took children and teachers on a 500-mile tour. Accommodation was provided at a hotel in Weston-super-Mare, 'a convenient centre for visiting Bath, Cheddar, Wells, Avonmouth Docks, a Somerset dairy farm etc'. Careful planning and classroom preparation beforehand became the prerequisites for success, with Mr Bryant giving such ventures his personal seal of approval by taking part himself in the excursion of 1960 to the Isle of Purbeck. This latter trip was recorded on 8mm colour film, in the form of an illustrated letter entitled 'Dear Mum', and became a feature of that summer's open day, when it proved, 'both amusing and instructive, and gave parents and visitors an opportunity to see how the week was spent'. Mr Bryant had in fact taken part in such excursions in the pre-war years and saw them as opportunities to, 'awaken a new enthusiasm following the more formal work preceding the Entrance Examination earlier in the year'.

Late June and early July was a time for one more round of term tests – and after they were marked the children were assigned their final position on the class list. Reports were written out and conveyed to each classroom in a large brown envelope, the arrival of which drew the attention of many pairs of anxious eyes. After their distribution the reports had then to go home, where the tally of each scholar's As, Bs and Cs, or otherwise, would receive its appropriate comment. And July was once again the occasion of another open afternoon for parents when they could discuss 'matters of an educational nature' (your marks!) with the teacher. But all might yet be well, for there was also a fine display of the school's needlework and handiwork, and to close the afternoon, a short musical performance by the children.

The new junior school's first open day was held in July 1953, and was well attended by parents who came to see their children's work: needlework, handwork, art, exercise books and examination papers ('worked scripts of tests by the children') were all put on display. During the afternoon 'a programme representative of a wide range of school activities was carried out by the children', and in the evening the school doors were opened again, 'to give fathers a better opportunity to attend; also mothers who were unable to come in the afternoon'. Mr Bryant, the new headteacher, was much encouraged by the interest it generated and open day became an annual fixture at Dollis Junior School, attended not only by parents but by other visitors too, among them members of the local education committee.

The annual Concert and Speech Day brought the year to a conclusion. Parents, together with a selection of Hendon officials, including the mayor and the chairman of the education committee, gathered in the school hall for a programme which included various performances by the children, the presentation of bouquets to the platform party, followed by awards and speeches. Tea and cakes in the staff room was the customary conclusion. The school doors closed for the summer vacation a day or two later.

MR BRYANT RETIRES

In 1963, after thirty-five years in the borough's service (and forty-one as a teacher), Mr Bryant retired. That October more than 250 parents, friends and former pupils turned out for a special ceremony at Dollis, to mark his retirement at the end of that month. His pupils gave him a garden voucher and a portable garden chair, and he was also presented with a barograph (a self-recording barometer), and also a television! Mr Bryant was proud of Dollis. It was, he felt, a school where the children were 'friendly and well behaved', where the relationship between pupils and teacher was 'a pleasing feature of the school', and where the co-operation and support of parents was 'very encouraging'. Forging a link between home and school, he thought, was essential, and to that end he had made himself, as headteacher, more accessible, setting aside a half day every week to see parents without any previous appointment. For their part, many parents had shown 'a keen interest' in the half-yearly reports which followed the school's own internal exams, and to Bryant this was clear evidence of the school's general success.

In its first years the new junior school had passed through some difficult times but it had eventually reached calmer waters – at least for the moment. Through it all Mr Bryant claimed to have experienced 'hardly a day's illness' and hoped to remain active in his retirement. 'I am proud', he had written in his very first report as headteacher at Dollis Junior School, 'to have had the honour to have been the first Head Teacher of the school'. It was his hope that the school 'will go from strength to strength and that all associated with the name Dollis will be proud of such association'.

Dollis in the 1960s and '70s

A NEW HEADTEACHER

Some forty-two applicants applied for Mr Bryant's position at Dollis, and in August 1963 Mr L.H. Patterson, then headmaster of North Harringay Junior School, Hornsey, was selected from a shortlist of five. Mr Bryant's resignation was to take effect from 31 October 1963, and as Mr Patterson was not able to take up his new post as headteacher at Dollis Junior School until 1 January 1964, the deputy headteacher at Dollis, Mr A.R. Thorpe, was appointed as acting headteacher for the interim (1 November to 31 December 1963).

Inevitably the appointment of a new headteacher brings with it change. In his first two terms at Dollis, Mr Patterson both made his own assessment of the school's strengths, weaknesses and 'potentialities', and also introduced certain 'innovations'. The school's curriculum was given a fresh look. The new headteacher oversaw the introduction of 'various new schemes of work', notably in science which, 'for the first time in this school', was to be taught as a subject in its own right. In introducing science as a separate subject, it was hoped to teach the children 'to observe, to question, to find the answers and to make simple deductions'. To this end, room 9, the general-purposes room, already used for individual science lessons, became an important teaching area for the new subject.

Dollis children were now to be more conversant with the language and methods of scientific enquiry, and they were also exposed for the first time to the teaching of a foreign language. In Mr Patterson's second term at Dollis, two 'colonial teachers' were temporarily at the school as staff replacements. As 'an experiment', one of them, Miss Lord, a French Canadian, was, 'used to give instruction in French to the top class'. Patterson thought it a success and wished to pursue it further. In the autumn of 1965 a short French course, with the emphasis 'on speech and conversation rather than a study of grammar,' was started for third- and fourth-year children. This was eventually developed, in 1972, into a three-year course taken by all children from the age of eight, who were to have three twenty-five-minute lessons per week. It was of course dependant on having the right teachers – in 1972 there were three able to share in French instruction, in 1975 there were four.

As the new headteacher was fond of music, this part of the curriculum was given a new emphasis. Being a player himself, he wished to see the children, 'make music rather than to be satisfied with the role of listeners'. To this end he started a recorder group and very soon had some forty young musicians performing at the morning assemblies, with plans to expand the group, its range of recorder types, and its repertoire in the following year. In 1965 the recorder group secured its first 'booking' with the Free church (just across the road from Dollis) to provide Christmas music, and rapidly established something of a local reputation. It was Mr Patterson's hope, as funding became available, to introduce violin instruction, and to eventually create a school orchestra. It was not, however, until September 1972 that the school was finally able to appoint a music specialist. The first incumbent, Miss T. Crowder, was at last able to provide the children with violin lessons, but in January 1974, though she continued to give weekly lessons, she was transferred to the borough's peripatetic staff. Her replacement, a professional singer, lasted a matter of weeks only, going absent in February before resigning in early March. 'Teaching', recorded Mr Patterson in his log book, 'affects her professional singing voice!'. Not until Mr H. Sowerby arrived in September 1974, as the school's new music specialist, did the aspiration of a real orchestra come to fruition. In March 1975 Mr Patterston and Mr Sowerby took eighty-nine Dollis children 'from the choir and orchestra' to a music festival at Moss Hall School. There were then ninety children learning and playing the recorder at Dollis, but also eighteen violinists, one flautist and two clarinet players.

Other of the new headteacher's 'innovations' involved the acquisition of new and more up-to-date resources and equipment for the school. In room 9, the general-purposes room, then being used as a school library, a reference library of some 300 books 'on Science, Geography, History, Mathematics and other subjects' was set up, in the hope of encouraging children, 'to carry out individual research and to find out information for themselves'. A television set was obtained for the school, and it, too, was put into room 9 where it joined the school's other 'teaching aids': the radio, sound and strip projectors and a tape recorder. The new television was soon made much use of, 'to obtain factual information on various subjects, and to provide a stimulus for oral and written english'.

Mr Patterson was keen to see Dollis play its part in the life of the local community. There was some concern, however, that as families grew up, 'the child-producing potential of the nearby estate [Brookfield] must fall'. This made it all the more important to draw children from other properties in the local area, yet there was evidence that some of these children were going elsewhere. In the hope of reversing such a trend and gathering the support of local parents and families, Patterson was soon pursuing the idea of creating a parent-teacher association, 'to give closer contact and a better understanding of our aims'. He had been much encouraged by the parental support and goodwill shown at the school's sports day and open evening, and in the spring of 1965 a Dollis PTA came into being. The following year the new PTA embarked on a major project that was to bring a new dimension to Dollis life: a learning swimming pool. In the process, the necessary fundraising was also to bring the school and the local community even closer together – in the very way that Mr Patterson had hoped for when he first took up the Dollis Junior headship.

RISING ROLLS AND MOBILE CLASSROOMS

Mr Patterson assumed the Dollis Junior headship with thirty years of teaching experience behind him, the last thirteen of which he had been a headteacher. He found a school with 320 children divided into ten classes. Eight of those classes were in the school's main building and two were in the HORSA hut. In the main building 'room 9' was retained for 'general purposes' (as originally designed), and also housed the school library. Apart from the headteacher, there were ten full-time teachers (one of whom was the deputy headteacher). Six teachers were women and four were men. The school roll had been down to this sort of level only since the autumn of 1961, and it was a considerable descent from the 511 reported in September 1955, when the school was described as 'filled to overflowing'. In 1964 the new headteacher had come to a school with the exact number of children for which it had been originally planned, but it was not to remain long in that happy state. Although initially the roll was to drop even further to 310 in September 1964, and to only 304 the following September, concern over falling numbers was quickly replaced by having to grapple with the problem of an imminent and major expansion of the local primary age population, the result of plans by the Ministry of Defence.

At nearby Inglis Barracks the MOD's expansion of the Army's married quarters soon had a marked effect on both Dollis Junior School and the Dollis Infant School. In the autumn of 1965 there were 192 houses in the course of construction at the barracks, and from the end of the year, and through the next two years, large numbers of army children were enrolled at the Dollis schools. The turnover was always high and over the next decade the 'barracks children' would come and go in considerable numbers. Moreover, these additional numbers now coming from the barracks would be swelled further by an upward swing in the general numbers of local primary-age children. By the start of the autumn term in 1966 the junior school roll was up to 353 but had reached more than 450 by the autumn of 1970. More classes had to be created, the teaching staff augmented and new accommodation found.

In the autumn of 1966 Patterson had eleven full-time teachers and two part-time (one of whom helped with the needlework classes). There was an additional, eleventh, class but it was forced to take up residence in the school medical room, as room 9 was still being retained for the library and general purposes. A mobile classroom was requested but did not arrive to alleviate the situation until the following June – and in September 1967 the crush of numbers was on again. The roll was up to 373, there were now twelve classes, and this time the extra classroom was found in the canteen at Canada Villa. In the headteacher's words, it was 'an enforced experiment' that proved 'a disaster'. The teacher and children had to carry their books and equipment across the playground each day as the canteen reverted to its intended function every evening. In September 1968, with the school roll standing at 395, the Canada Villa experiment finally came to an end when a second mobile classroom was set up between the second- and third-year corridors. It was joined there by the first mobile classroom, which was moved from its original position in the corner of the playground (now the Elsie Henderson Corner), in order to make way for the intended school swimming pool.

By the autumn of 1970 the school roll had risen to 452. There were thirteen full-time teachers, besides the headteacher, and three more working part-time. To accommodate yet another new class, Mr Patterson had to resort finally to room 9, hitherto kept apart for general purposes and the library. Reluctantly it was turned into a regular classroom, its library books being transferred to the corridors.

In January 1971 another full-time teacher was added to the staff, which allowed the creation of a further class. Mr Patterson used the opportunity to make four classes for his third-year children (year-five children in today's parlance), as these children had been in three classes of some forty-three in each, ever since leaving the infant school. From the autumn of 1972 the junior school's fourteen classes were to be found in the nine classrooms of the main building, in the two HORSA classrooms, and in the mobile classrooms, of which there were now three for an additional one had been acquired from the infant school (near the end of the second-year corridor), as the infant school was then having two new mobile classrooms erected over the old air-raid shelters near its dining hall. With this final addition received from the infant school, Dollis Junior School's need for accommodation found a solution which was to last for the next twenty years.

The number of children fell off gradually. In the autumn of 1974 it stood at 394, divided among thirteen classes, which allowed the recently acquired mobile classroom from the infant school to become the music room. In September 1977, at the start of Mr Patterson's last year as headteacher, the junior school roll was down to 356.

HEAVING FLOORS, BURSTING PIPES AND … PAINTERS!

In September 1964 Mr Patterson submitted a report for the attention of the borough's Engineer and Surveyor's Department, 'concerning certain works of maintenance and repair which required attention' – and not so very long afterwards he had still more to add to it. By the time he came to submit his second formal report on the school, in November 1965, Patterson was expressing concern over the 'undue amount of attention' he was giving to the repair and maintenance of the school building. Security, or rather the lack of it, was a particularly worrying problem, as sections of the fence alongside the railway and surrounding the playing field were either in a state of disrepair or entirely missing! At weekends and on evenings, 'youths' invaded the school grounds and were even to be found on the roofs. Classroom windows were being broken and the school was 'frequently burgled' as window catches and door locks were either missing or vandalised. Complaints over the same went back at least three years. Much of this was in fact improved over the course of the following year but the gremlins which seem to inhabit some buildings are never idle for long!

In June 1965 the hall floor, of laid wooden blocks, had begun 'erupting', swelling up, with large sections of the blocks being displaced. Despite attempts to repair it, the problem persisted over the next two years, each renewal being followed by another eruption. The hall was put out of use for much of the 1966/67 academic year, causing considerable inconvenience. Trouble, however, seems to like company, and concurrent with the school's floor trouble came a leaking roof. Rain got into the cloakrooms and the long cross-corridor. While men were at work in the hall, others were repairing the roof, and for good measure the borough was also having the school redecorated! The autumn of 1966 was a particularly trying time for not only was much of school life being disrupted by workmen, but the rising number of children in the school was becoming a real problem. The mobile classroom requested that September did not arrive until June, and in the meantime the school's medical room had to do duty as a classroom.

As will be seen, such periods of minor crisis have been an almost regularly recurring feature of Dollis life – a legacy of the circumstances of the school's original construction. Following that of 1966, burst pipes, boiler problems, a run of broken windows and forced doors (the work of vandals), and a reappearance of the leaks ('numerous') in the roof of the long cross-corridor, filled in the time until the next major convergence of such troubles produced another period of minor crisis and notable mayhem – not that the children were much bothered! Nine years on, in October 1975, the decorators turned up again – always an ominous sign it seems – and began what turned out to be a very long campaign with bucket and brush which took them through to the end of February before the final stroke was applied. To accommodate them, the classes were moved in turn into the music room, while music lessons were taken in the hall, and PE lessons restricted to only one per class each week.

The painters had hardly begun when in November roofing contractors arrived to begin the replacement of the perspex roofing on the classroom corridors … and more trouble was brewing underground. Excessive condensation was noticed in the switch room (next to the medical room), and over the next few days a series of burst pipes made themselves all too evident under the new swimming pool changing rooms, in the entrance foyer and along the corridor between the foyer and the long cross-corridor. The hot water pipes supplying the staff toilets failed and at the end of the month a gale blew off the roofing from four classrooms. It was not a happy time! With perhaps a touch of understatement, Mr Patterson noted in his log book that, 'Plumbers (complete with drills), painters and roofing contractors have almost taken possession of the building'.

The decorating continued over the Christmas holiday, but when the headteacher returned in January he found not only fresh paint, but also new damage – for further gales (recorded nationally at up to 105mph) had torn away more of the school's roofing. The painters carried on, at one stage forcing the headteacher out of his own room and into the school office, and did not complete their appointed task until the end of February, some four-and-a-half months after they had begun! With this latest round of decorating over, the school settled back to the more usual routine of the occasional leaking pipe and bursting boiler … and wayward window cleaners. The latter it seems, caused Mr Patterson considerable irritation on several occasions!

DOLLIS GETS A SWIMMING POOL

All of the worry over the foregoing tended to pale by comparison to that involved in taking on the construction of a Dollis Junior swimming pool … and in maintaining it. In March 1965 an open meeting of parents resolved to form a parent/teacher association (PTA), and that May the new association held its first committee meeting. One of the association's aims was to raise funds for the school, and over the years its support enabled the purchase of stage curtains and black-out curtains for the hall and equipment for the school office. Very early in its existence it became involved in one major project that was to consume much of its energy.

In July 1966 a PTA sub-committee was set up to explore the possibility of building a school swimming pool, a 'learner pool'. That autumn the association's annual general meeting resolved to raise the necessary money for the project, a decision which launched it into a series of fundraising activities that soon broadened into a community effort. A jumble sale that December raised £120 and was followed by a summer fayre which netted a profit of £529, and an Easter bazaar in 1968 which brought in another £181, all for the pool fund. Members of the local Free church, with others from Canada Villa, made a donation from the receipts taken for a series of one-act plays. In December 1967 members of the Canada Villa youth club put on a pantomime which raised another £100 for the pool. There were sales of 'old woollens', and a barn dance. Former pupils like Alison Wray (1967-71) recall what seemed to them to be 'ages raising money for it'. Graham Hunt (1964-68) remembers doing 'lots of fundraising' but sadly left the school (July 1968) before the pool was built.

As originally planned, the pool was to be covered, and built in the playground 'alongside the verandah' outside of the hall, i.e. adjacent to the hall terrace. This, however, was objected to by the borough's planning department and, instead, at Mr Patterson's suggestion, it was built in the inset corner of the playground bounded by the end of the hall, the medical room and one of the covered play areas – now the Elsie Henderson Corner. The new site, being over the school's main drains, meant that the drains had to be strengthened and the pool raised. Excavation commenced in September 1968. The shell of the pool was soon finished and most of the work completed by the end of November. On 3 May 1969 the pool was officially opened by the Mayor of Barnet, and in June the PTA put on a second summer fayre, which was opened by the president of the Barnet Amateur Swimming Association. The pool was an immediate success, both junior and infant children making use of it, and the headteacher soon reporting, 'some 1,300 children passing through it each week'. Almost all of the junior school's children would learn to swim by the time they left Dollis.

Fundraising for the pool continued, but the following year the intended second phase of the project, to cover the pool, was deferred indefinitely due to cost (estimated at £5,500). Instead, attention turned to converting the former covered play area, adjacent to the pool, into changing rooms. The borough architect drew up plans, and it was hoped that some assistance with the cost would be forthcoming, but this was not to be. Despite the fact that the borough had assumed responsibility for pool maintenance and repairs from November 1970, it was left to the school to find the money for the changing rooms, initially estimated at £2,000. The PTA was again committed to raising funds – and in the meantime the children had to make do with the lavatories as changing rooms, a situation which caused great concern, especially in the spring of 1973 when there was an outbreak of dysentery at the school. Not until 1974 was the project given formal approval, and only in June 1975 did construction, with prefabricated sections, begin, the work being finally finished in October. The final cost was just under £1,000, all of it raised by the PTA.

Swimming instruction in the new pool began in May 1970, on three days a week, with an instructor supplied by the borough. The aim was to teach the children to swim at least 25 yards by the time they left the school. The pool was popular, not least with those staff who enjoyed swimming, but the abiding memory of many children was of a pool that was frequently 'freezing'. Swimming started in the summer term, at the beginning of May, temperature permitting! Every year during the summer term there was a sponsored swim to raise money for charity, and for the pool and changing rooms fund – in June 1975 it raised £250. Swimming resumed briefly in the autumn term, and continued until cold weather brought it to a chilly end! Being outdoors the pool was subject to all the whims of weather, despite its heater. The freak summer weather of 1975 dropped pool temperatures into the 50°s F, while the heatwave of the following summer saw them soar to 80°F.

Apart from the weather, one of the other problems with open-air pools is security. In July 1977 a meeting was held at the town hall to discuss this problem. It was one of particular concern to the Dollis headteacher, as local 'louts and vandals' had become a serious nuisance. Break-ins were then occurring almost nightly, and every weekend. The previous year the pool had suffered seven such assaults in one weekend; on the Sunday afternoon the new changing rooms had been entered and 'fouled … dog like!'. With the police and the council seemingly unable to prevent it, Mr Patterson resorted to draining the pool each summer as 'a defensive measure'. It was a sad state of affairs, and the pool's wooden fence enclosure would eventually acquire a topping of barbed wire. And all of this was added to the list of repairs necessary to keep the pool going – repairs to the heating system, replacement of the motor and pump when they unexpectedly burnt out. The creation and continuance of the Dollis swimming pool demanded considerable persistence.

MANAGERS

Mr Patterson's arrival at Dollis Junior School in 1964 coincided with a major reorganisation of metropolitan local government. The GLC (Greater London Council) was in the process of creation (to emerge in 1965) and with it came the new London Borough of Barnet. Teachers and schools were inevitably affected. The various Hendon teachers' associations disappeared as a Barnet Teachers' Association, and a Barnet Head Teachers' Conference, were formed. The new Dollis Junior head himself became a member of the Block Allowance working party, set up to advise the new Borough of Barnet on capitation allowances. The school was put under a new system of management, becoming one in a group of schools placed under the direction of a single managing body, in which borough councillors played a prominent part. The statutory obligation to create 'Managing Bodies for County Primary Schools' had been deferred in Middlesex from 1961, but with the reorganisation of local government in 1965, twelve such bodies were established to govern the new Borough of Barnet's sixty-seven primary schools. Each group consisted of from four to seven schools, and was run by a management board composed largely of local councillors and their political associates, many of whom commonly served on the boards of two or more groups. Headteachers might attend, but did not have a right to do so. It was a situation which gave rise to criticism, prompting the suggestion that such bodies lacked dedication and rigor. From 1971 there was a nominal parental presence on managing bodies, and from 1975 it was resolved in principle that parental representation be extended, that teachers should be represented and that whenever possible each primary school should have a separate managing body.

Dollis Junior School was one of four schools belonging to group XI, the others being Dollis Infant, Courtland Junior Mixed and Infant and the Fairway Junior Mixed and Infant schools. Mr Patterson regularly attended the managing body's termly meetings (held in rotation at the various schools in the group), as he did the meetings of the various teachers' and headteachers' associations. In the summer term the school would receive a visit from its managers, as they carried out their annual inspection of the school buildings.

TEACHERS

Temporary absences and a regular turnover in the teaching staff are things that headteachers must confront. Indeed Mr Patterson's predecessor, Mr Bryant, had perhaps more than his share of such difficulties in the 1950s, the result of, 'promotion, marriage, removal and other factors'. In 1971 Mr Patterson lost six of his teachers to all too familiar causes: 'babies, changes in husband's employment and one promotion'.

In order to make good any temporary absences from among his full-time teaching staff, Mr Patterson could draw upon his part-time staff members – and in this regard the school had frequent recourse to one of its part-timers in particular, Mrs Barbara Simons. With only one or two such staff members, however, this was a very limited resource, and beyond it the headteacher was dependent on the borough's general reserve of supply teachers. Moreover, he was also reliant on the borough to fill vacancies in his teaching staff. The problem was that the Borough of Barnet, in common with other local authorities in London, was experiencing increasing difficulties in finding teachers, supply or full-time. This was hardly a new difficulty, and its persistent recurrence has continued to be a particularly knotty problem for London schools.

Teachers found London to be too expensive. In 1967 there was a reported 'drift' of newly qualified teachers away from Barnet into other areas where housing was more affordable. In his annual report on Dollis, presented in November 1972, Mr Patterson noted that staff turnover continued to be high, four of his teachers having left in the past year, 'to secure cheaper accommodation outside London'. In 1973 the borough's education committee heard that the current level of house prices was hampering both the recruitment and the retention of experienced teachers, and that there was a lack of interest in vacancies for head and deputy headteachers. A petition, signed by 1,635 of the borough's teachers was submitted by the Barnet Teachers' Council. Teachers wanted an immediate increase to their London allowance, raising it from £118 to £300 per year. The borough tried various remedies – separation allowances, temporary housing, help with removal and mortgage costs – and considered others, but any lasting solution remained elusive.

In a general climate of trade-union unrest across the country, and against a local situation described as 'steadily worsening', teachers' unions took strike action. In February 1969, NAS (National Association of Schoolmasters) members held a half-day strike, but in November the whole of the Dollis Junior School staff, on instructions from their various unions, walked out, closing the school for a day. In January 1970 there was a far more serious disruption when the headteacher, Mr Patterson, his deputy headteacher, and eleven other NUT (National Union of Teachers) members took part in a strike which closed the school for two weeks. That June there was another day long walk out by NAS members. In March 1973, the headteacher and nine other teachers at the school joined another NUT strike day, called to protest the collapse of negotiations over the London allowance. The deputy headteacher, with the four remaining teachers, came in to teach – only four classes were held. Staff shortages, however, continued. In May 1974 Mr Patterson was 'warning' of possible strike action at Dollis due to staffing problems – a vacancy which occurred in February had not been filled, and the school was currently short four teachers, with Mrs Simons filling in full-time all week. In July, NUT members walked out again.

SCHOOL DAYS

Memories of school days depend of course on your vantage point … and your personal point of view! Mr Charles Thornton, who taught at Dollis Junior School from 1954 until he left in 1967 to become deputy headteacher at Holly Park School, Friern Barnet, recalls a school which had 'a nice atmosphere', in which there was 'good discipline' and 'well-behaved pupils'. Corporal punishment (with slipper and cane) from the headteacher was still a possibility, and though rarely resorted to, its lingering threat did leave a distinct and lasting impression on many of those who viewed 'behaviour' and 'discipline' from the opposite end of the cane, so to speak! To pupils, the headteacher, Mr Patterson, and other teachers too, seemed 'very strict' - from the latter a slap on bare legs, or a ruler across the hands, was still a possibility. Mr Patterson 'ran a tight ship', an impression certainly conveyed to young minds as he routinely entered assemblies carrying his cane. Nonetheless, if assemblies were somewhat formal, with a scripture lesson (read by the headteacher), prayers and a hymn, there were also the playlets of the Friday morning 'goody-goody' assemblies, when each week the classes took it in turn to lead an assembly. In their classrooms the children sat at desks arranged precisely in rows, and facing the front. Respect for elders demanded that all stand when the headteacher entered the assembly hall, and when any teacher entered the classroom. Boys wore short trousers, and the school's dress code was enforced with few concessions. Yet with these memories are also those of 'a happy school', a 'very encouraging school' in which many teachers showed a real interest in their children.

Half-yearly, in February, and again at the end of the year in July, each child took home their 'Scholars Report Book'. A grade was assigned for each subject studied: religious knowledge, reading, English (grammar and comprehension), handwriting, spelling, composition, mathematics (tables, mental and arithmetic), science, geography, history, art, craft and physical training, and there were also remarks on progress in music. In their second year they started learning French. Opposite the list of grades, the teacher had a space for general remarks. Each pupil was assigned a position in their class according to their grades, which made for very keen competition, and not a little worry over dropping a place! In the final year of primary school there was the matter of 'secondary transfer', making that step up from primary to secondary school. The anxiety of this particular rite of passage, especially for those children who were hoping for a grammar school place, was underscored by the ordeal of those tests and essays which constituted the '11-plus'. Children who were going on to local schools, like Copthall or Edgware, might be taken on a visit to their next school, and several of the local headteachers also came to Dollis to talk to the final-year pupils.

Parents were afforded the opportunity to scrutinise the progress of their offspring at Dollis at the school's open evenings. Following an agreement made with the borough's education officer in 1964, primary schools were to hold at least one open evening each year to, 'enable parents to see the work and discuss the progress of their children with the teachers'. At Dollis such evenings occurred twice yearly, in October and in July.

The influx of children from Inglis Barracks increased the need at Dollis for remedial teaching, as, 'owing to frequent changes of school, the children from the Barracks are invariably below our own children in attainments'. Their needs could only be met by remedial teaching in groups. Mr Patterson felt that his staff could cope with the teaching problem, but needed additional accommodation. For those with reading problems there had long been remedial reading lessons at Dollis, and from March 1973 Dollis also became the site of one of the Borough of Barnet's remedial reading centres – located in a mobile classroom (latterly the 'Steel Pans' Hut'), newly planted in a corner of the lower playground, directly across from the site of the swimming pool. From 1975, sixth-form girls from neighbouring Copthall School started coming to Dollis to help teachers in the lower school with reading lessons. Their arrival coincided with concerns expressed by the borough's director of educational services over the need for more centrally-based remedial teachers, to cope with the increased number of children with social and learning problems, and in particular to assist the many non-English speaking immigrant children, whose numbers were on the increase. Indeed, from the late 1960s the borough had been developing a remedial education service, a process spurred along by Government legislation which, from April 1971, required that no child be left outside of the educational system. Previously such children as were deemed 'unsuitable for education in school' had been the responsibility of the Local Health Authority. The Education (Handicapped Children) Act 1970, passed that charge over to local education authorities.

KEEPING HEALTHY – MEDICALS, MILK AND A BREAK!

The school routine included regular medical checks, for which purpose there was a medical room and an appointed school doctor. In the 1950s school-age children were given a general medical examination as 'entrants' at five/six years of age, with further routine examinations at age eight/nine years and '10 years plus', and finally as 'leavers' (age fifteen, raised to sixteen in 1973). By the early 1960s, however, this traditional pattern, then over fifty years old, was being modified as more recent evidence showed that children were generally in much better health, and suffered from a comparatively small number of problems than had previously been true. Moreover it was felt that the National Health Service now offered ample facilities for detection and treatment. The intermediate examination at age eight/nine years was thought unnecessary by many local authorities, being replaced by regular visits by the school doctor to discuss particular children whom teachers were concerned about. An intermediate examination for the age group '10 plus', however, was kept. In addition health visitors paid regular visits to check on cleanliness and eyesight, while school doctors made regular inspections of School Meals Service kitchens and dining halls. A school dentist came to inspect teeth and oral hygiene, and an audiometrician came to test the children's hearing.

The Dollis medical room was kept busy as the venue for about ten medial inspections and tests every year. The round of examinations included general medicals, dental inspections, eye tests, the occasional foot inspection, hygiene inspections and hearing tests with the audiometrician and her machine. There were medical examinations for the school-journey parties, and periodic head inspections – children found with nits were excluded from school until given the all-clear by the school medical officer. Occasionally there were visits from an outside psychologist (from University College Hospital for example) to see or discuss those children who had behavioural problems.

Fresh air, exercise and a daily ration of milk were also deemed important for good health. Break times were an important part of the school day. Jill Vinson (Valentine, 1971-76) remembers playing British bulldog and doing handstands in the shelters, 'ball against the wall games', playing marbles on the drains, skipping games and jumping games with the 'elastic'. 'Two balls' was another favourite. At the first break there was also free milk (introduced in 1944) but this was an indulgence nearing its end. For junior school children it was last drunk in 1971. There were no longer compelling medical reasons to keep it. Primary-age children were much healthier, and in general were thought to derive little real benefit. Of 36,000 children of all ages examined in Barnet over a three-year period, 1968-70, only twenty-six had been found to have an unsatisfactory physical condition, and of those twenty-five were given a certificate for free milk. By the Education (milk) Act, 1971, local authorities were obliged to supply free milk only to school children up to age seven, to pupils in special schools and to those children who the school medical officer certified as needing it. Whatever the children might have thought, overall there was little parental reaction to the withdrawal, though the GLC did make an attempt to circumvent what they claimed was 'an anti-social act'.

MUSIC, SPORTS AND CLASS OUTINGS

Music features in the recollections of many past pupils, and was one of the headteacher's special interests. The school had a choir, an orchestra, a country-dance team and a recorder group. The latter was run by Mr Patterson himself, and regularly provided the music for the annual carol service at the local Free church across the road from Dollis. The school's musicians also supported Christmas services at the Union church. Alison Wray recalls that when her year arrived at the junior school, Mr Patterson had decided not to give recorder lessons, '... but we pestered and pestered till he gave in. We soon joined the full recorder group and played fabulous part music such as the *Dambusters' March* and *Elizabethan Serenade*'. Dollis Junior parents were regularly treated to two school concerts – in December there was an evening carol service by the choir and orchestra, and another evening of performances in the summer term, in July. There was a special Jubilee Concert in June 1977, the year of both the Queen's and the school's silver jubilee. From time to time Dollis received visits from other musical groups. Very soon after Mr Patterson's arrival at Dollis, the Camden Players were invited to put on a concert of recorder music for the children. There were special evening concerts too – one by the Ionian Dance Group and Choir, another by the Brimsley Singers. The Barnet Quartet, the Graham Park School Band and an operatic group from Southgate Technical College were other visitors to Dollis.

Dollis' young musicians made their own musical excursions too. They were regular participants in the various music and dance festivals held at local schools. In March 1975 the music teacher, Mr H. Sowerby, took a large contingent of eighty-nine children (choir and orchestra) to a music festival at Moss Hall School, and that summer took the orchestra on the first of two visits to the Royal Military School of Music at Kneller Hall. There was also a visit to the BCC for eight lucky members of the orchestra, and in March 1977 Mr Sowerby and two parents took sixteen members of the orchestra on a four-day trip into Wales to give a series of concerts. Nor were immediate neighbours forgotten: Dollis singers and musicians entertained the members of the local Darby and Joan Club at the Free church across the road, went next door to play for the infants, and down Pursley Road to play their violins at Copthall.

Sports also played an important part in school life. Alison Wray remembers the very keen competition between the Dollis houses at the school's own sports day – and her own attempts to win extra points for Wilberforce! Vivette (1970-74) and Juliette Robinson (1972-76) have special reasons to recall their sporting days at Dollis. In 1974 Vivette's personal successes in the athletics competitions at the inter-schools sports made the local newspaper. Juliette followed her elder sister with her own achievements, and well remembers being Nicoll's captain in 1976 when it won the school's sports-day cup.

Sports came to the fore especially during the summer term. The school continued to hold its own annual inter-house sports day, but the Hendon inter-schools sports days held at the Burroughs were replaced by competition in the new Borough of Barnet's West District Athletics, held at the new Copthall Stadium (opened in 1964). The school enjoyed a number of notable sporting achievements. The Dollis girls came away with first place in the Barnet West District inter-schools athletics in 1973, 1974 and 1976. The school's swimmers took first place in the swimming gala of 1967, tied for the same with Colindale in 1971, and again swam their way to a first place in 1978 in the first inter-schools gala held at the new Copthall pool (opened in 1977). The Boys' football team won Hendon's Northern Section Championship in 1964 and were runners-up in the Hendon Championship. Two years later they won the Douglas Martin Cup (for Barnet's West District), and did the same again the following year in April 1967. In 1976 they shared the Martin Cup with Edgware, and the next year won it outright, also playing in the regional final.

Sports got a special boost at local schools in July 1964 when the All England Sports was held at the new Copthall stadium, and again in the summer of 1977 when Copthall was the venue for the English Schools Athletics Championship. Dollis parents acted as hosts for some of the competitors on both occasions, and in 1964 the school itself was used as a meals centre, charged with feeding some 260 competitors each evening. In 1977 two of the school's teachers were attached to the Warwickshire party as guides.

Lessons in the classroom were supplemented by class outings, and in the summer term by extended school journeys for the older children in the two upper years. Day visits took in local businesses such as the Moat Mount Dairy. Venturing further afield there were trips to Windsor Safari Park, to St Albans, Whipsnade, Hatfield House, Hampton Court, Kew Gardens, the London Planetarium and the Tower of London. The older children visited various London museums, and occasionally there was something special. In 1964 children in their final year at Dollis were taken by the headteacher on a trip to Windsor by steamer and train. The highlight of the year, however, came in the summer term, when school journey parties set out for more distant destinations. There were usually two such parties (each of thirty to forty children, accompanied by three teachers), made up from the children in the upper years. The children taking part were away for a full seven-day week, and preceding each journey they were given a medical examination, often the day before departure. The Isle of Wight (Sandown and Shanklin) was the most frequent destination, followed by Teignmouth and Swanage, but there were also forays to Lyme Regis, Coventry, Cromer and Hythe. Despite the best efforts of teachers, pupils don't always remember the educational bits the most – Graham Hunt (1964-68) recalls the nightly squabbles in a Shanklin hotel over which of the four boys in his room would be forced to share the double bed!

FIRE, BOMBS, POWER CUTS AND ROYAL DIVERSIONS

If there was a routine to school life, there were also special occasions ... and the unexpected! In January 1968 overnight snow brought traffic to a standstill. The school did not close, but attendance figures plummeted – only 239 children out of 382 attended. The snow stayed on the ground for about six days, its presence apparently suggesting a tempting reason for missing school. Attendance figures improved only gradually, but in February they were dealt another blow by an outbreak of flu. That month nine teachers went absent. In 1976 there was a repeat, with the school in the throes of another February flu epidemic which lasted a full month, and some months later, in June, the temperature began to climb. In the mobile huts it reached into the 90s and in early July went up to 100°F. A class visit to Whipsnade was cut short because of the extreme heat. If snow was distracting Dollis' young scholars in January 1968, eight-and-a-half years later it was unbearable heat! The drought experienced that summer was declared to be the longest in 250 years, and was not officially over until mid-November. Indeed 1976 was the second of two consecutive years of freakish weather. The year before there had been balmy summer weather in January, snow in early June, and finally a heat wave!

Human agency, even that of very small humans, can wreak havoc with the best-laid plans of teachers. On 20 June 1968, in the early afternoon, at the height of a thunderstorm, fire broke out in the store room of the Dollis Infant School. With a blaze well under way, and smoke soon billowing from the roof, some 380 infant children were led out into the playing fields, where heavy rain soon forced them indoors again – into the hall of the junior school! Anxious parents were soon arriving in numbers, but their worst fears proved unfounded. The Mill Hill Fire Brigade were quickly on hand to prevent the fire spreading, and there were no injuries. Despite first suspicions turning to the possibility of a lightning strike, the finger of blame soon pointed to the handiwork of two of the infant children themselves. In Mr Patterson's laconic account, 'Two Infant children set fire to the Infants School …'! It was an afternoon of much excitement … and disruption at both schools, but fortunately there was no unrepairable damage or loss of life.

In January 1976, however, there was an incident which had the potential to become something very serious indeed. At ten past two in the afternoon of the sixteenth, against a background of several very recent IRA bombings in London, Mr Patterson received a phone message informing him that there was a bomb in the junior school, and that he had half-an-hour to clear the building! Considering the school's proximity to Inglis Barracks, and the number of army children attending Dollis, it could indeed be a very real threat. The police were informed immediately and the children evacuated. The building remained empty until 3 p.m., the end of the normal afternoon break. This was excitement indeed … and fortunately nothing more than that!

Less dramatic than fires and bombs, but just as disruptive were power cuts and fuel shortages. The 1970s were a time of discontent, dispute and strike for many of Britain's workers (including teachers). In December of 1970, a succession of power cuts, the result of strike action by power workers, hit the school, causing cancellation of two of that year's Christmas concerts, there were concerts planned that year for each year group. Little over a year later, in February 1972, a miners' strike led to further power cuts, as the country was plunged into a state of emergency and a three-day working week for industry in order to conserve coal supplies.

The discontent among miners and power workers was not easily assuaged, and in November 1973 an even more serious situation developed when coal miners and power workers again started an industrial action which lead to another state of emergency and a three-day working week across the country. Coinciding with an Arab oil embargo, the fall out of another Arab-Israeli conflict (the Yom Kippur War), Britain soon found itself in a full-blown fuel crisis. At Dollis teachers and children soon felt the effects. The use of electricity for heating was put under restriction, and those in the mobile huts suffered the consequences, but the main school building soon felt the pinch too, when a compulsory 10 per cent reduction in fuel consumption was imposed. The school had changed over from coal to oil fired boilers in 1968, and at the end of November, when extremely cold weather coincided with the fuel cuts, the temperature dropped to only 49°F in the coldest parts of the building. And as the temperature dropped so too did attendance. On 30 November there were 110 absentees from a roll of 388. The cold weather and the heating economies continued, and on 18 December instructions were received to close the school that day for the term because of the fuel shortage.

Imagine then, the headteacher's surprise when the very next day, at 7.30 a.m., fuel oil was delivered to the school! That morning 150 children showed up, their 'voluntary attendance' qualifying them for a Dollis Christmas dinner. Staff were present too, and all went home only after a full plate of Christmas fare! The school closed for the Christmas break, but the fuel economy regulations were still in force when teachers and children returned in January.

Fortunately the gloom of power cuts, strikes and fuel shortages, was given some relief in the form of extra, and unique, holidays. Royal occasions have always blessed the British school child's calendar with holidays, and the 1970s provided several. In November 1972 there was a holiday to celebrate the Queen's twentieth wedding anniversary, and on 14 November 1973 (the very day before the order restricting the use of electricity) the school was closed for HRH Princess Anne's wedding to Captain Mark Phillips. In June 1977 there was time off for the Queen's Silver Jubilee, also commemorated that October by a special planting of six silver birch trees at Dollis – it was also the school's own silver jubilee. By way of historical note there was also a half-day holiday in 1965, on 25 June, to celebrate the 750th anniversary of the signing of the Magna Carta!

CHANGING HEADS

In March 1978, at the end of the spring term, Mr Patterson retired from the Dollis Junior headship. He had been a teacher for forty-five years, the last twenty-seven of those as a headteacher, of which fourteen years were spent at Dollis Junior School.

On his last day he was in reflective mood, recalling that time in 1933 when he had first become a teacher. The country was then in a state of economic depression, and teachers' salaries (£192 per year in London, £180 elsewhere) were cut by 10 per cent. Now, in March 1978 it seemed as if the wheel had come full circle. 'As I bow out', he noted, 'sanctions are being imposed to enforce a claim for an additional 10%'.

Earlier in the month, Mr D.A. Heasman, the new headteacher-elect since February, had made the first of half a dozen visits to Dollis in preparation for taking over the headship. Apart from talking to the staff and to the children, he also interviewed applicants for the post of school secretary, and visited the infant school. As Mr Heasman would not be able to assume his new post until September, Mr Peter Joy, the deputy headteacher (since 1972) stood in as acting headteacher for the summer term.

In his first school newsletter of September 1978, Mr Heasman noted down his impressions of Dollis Junior School as Mr Patterson had left it. The new headteacher found the school to be well organised, giving the children a secure environment. The children were controlled and seemed generally well behaved in school, at playtime and at home time. The children were proud of their school, a pride which Mr Heasman thought had, 'undoubtedly been largely brought about by Mr Patterson's firm insistence that all children wear school uniform and boys wear short trousers.' The school had a strong teaching staff, well supported by the school secretary, the welfare officer, the caretaker and the cook supervisor. The children enjoyed an excellent range of opportunities for music and for sports. The school meals were 'excellent'. The building and facilities seemed 'first class'. It was a school that was clean, well maintained and 'cared for'.

Canada Villa,
c. 1962.
(*Hendon Times*)

Dollis
Council
Junior and
Infant School,
summer 1939.

Front
entrance,
Dollis Junior
School.

Lower playground, Elsie
Henderson Corner and hall,
2003.

Elsie Henderson Corner,
April 1999.

HORSA hut, erected in
1947/48, used by juniors
from 1948-93.

Mobile classrooms, 1966/67.

Headmaster H.E. Bryant (centre), October 1963. (*Hendon Times*)

Summer Fayre, June 1967. (*Hendon Times*)

Above: Official opening of training pool by the Mayor of Barnet, 3 May 1969. Headmaster L.H. Patterson is in a dark suit directly behind the boy in the pool. (*Hendon Times*)

Right: Elsie Henderson, 'Lollipop of the Year', July 1975, with Sarah Rhodes (right) and Elaine Dickson. (*Hendon Times*)

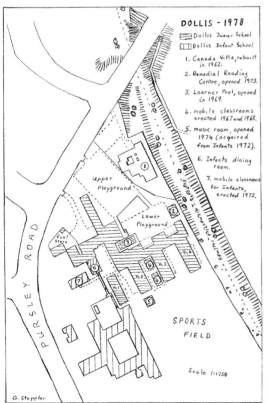

Above: Mr A. Leigh with Martin Cup winners, July 1967.

Left: Dollis, 1978.

CHANGING TIMES:
1978 ONWARDS

MAKING CHANGES – A NEW HEADTEACHER

The new headteacher, Mr D.A. Heasman, had begun his teaching career in 1954 at the Oliver Goldsmith Junior School in Kingsbury. Subsequently he had been deputy headteacher at Kingsbury Green JMI School, and in 1968 had been appointed as the first headteacher of Bedmond JMI School (then still under construction) near Abbots Langley. In February 1978 he was selected as the new Dollis Junior School headteacher, after what he recalled as a memorable evening spent at Hendon Town Hall. He and five other short-listed candidates (who included Mr Peter Joy, then deputy head of Dollis), were each subjected to interview, in time-honoured fashion, by an array of councillors and education officers.

As a new headteacher, Mr D.A. Heasman brought to Dollis his energy and enthusiasm, and a new approach to managing the school's affairs. Dollis had always had close links with the local community, but the new headteacher wished to stimulate further the relationship between parents, school, teachers and children, creating a school where all felt 'part of one big team/family … working together for the common good of the children'. To this end, in October 1978, only weeks after commencing his headship, he sought and obtained the disbandment of the school's PTA, preferring, as he explained, to get *all* parents involved, 'rather than just the members of a small committee'. Indeed he was later to dismiss the Dollis PTA in the most disparaging and uncharitable terms, claiming it to have been 'run by a white middle class English clique who … had raised pennies rather than pounds'. Perhaps it is not so surprising, as he himself later recalled, that he felt that he 'was not well accepted!'. Instead of working through the PTA he intended to make direct use of that goodwill that many parents quite naturally show towards the school that teaches their children. Personal, direct appeals and regular communication with parents, especially via a school 'newsletter', were central to this approach.

The headteacher sought both practical assistance and financial help. The recruitment of willing parents began immediately – resiting and rewiring the school kiln (delivered in 1974 but still not in use) and the pin boarding of the entrance lobby, hall and main corridors, became the first of many projects which would be carried out by parent volunteers over the ensuing years. A School Fund was set up and fundraising assumed a much more prominent place in school life. It was always aimed at specific goals: the purchase of rucksacks for school journeys and educational visits, the creation of a new library and the purchase of books to fill it, were among the very first.

The headteacher led the way with a Christmas Bazaar in November 1978, aimed specifically at raising money to purchase rucksacks for use on school journeys. In March 1979 he led a chartered train trip to York – 'the Dollis Special' – which took children, their families and teachers (some 300 passengers in all) northwards on a day excursion which was an enjoyable social occasion, an educational visit to an historic English city – and a fundraising venture for the school. The trip was deemed a great success, and although the profits fell far short of what had been hoped for, the venture was tried again in 1983. The Christmas Bazaar became an annual event, at first held on a weekday immediately after school, it had moved to a Saturday by 1987, and in 1994 became part of a fun day which came to include a morning of netball and football matches involving teachers, parents and governors, followed by lunch. In 1989 and 1990 there was no Christmas Bazaar. In March 1991 there was a Spring Fayre instead, followed in November by a bazaar held jointly with the infant school. The idea of holding a Summer Fête was explored briefly in 1982, but this particular venture had to wait until June 1984, after which it became a regular fundraising event, held every second year. The 'traditional' annual sponsored swim in the Dollis pool was continued, the takings being divided between the annual Mayor's Charity and the new School Fund – the swim of 1984 was missed out on account of the Summer Fête. Dollis became the first winner of the Mayor's Charity Shield (established in 1979), for its contribution of £350 to that year's appeal for Multiple Sclerosis.

The link with the local Darby and Joan Club for the elderly, which met at the Free church, continued too for a time. Food gifts, donated for the school's annual harvest assembly held in October, were distributed to its members, and were also taken to the elderly residents of the Moreton Close home, and to the Convent of St Mary at the Cross, Edgware, for disabled children. In June 1979 the headteacher and his wife treated club members to a 'mystery coach drive', hosted by his senior pupils and paid for out of the new School Fund. By 1985, however, a decision was made to make a 'break' with the 'traditional' harvest assembly. Instead of distributing food gifts locally, to people 'who in some cases don't need it or appreciate it', it was decided to take part in the 'Band Aid Schools for Africa Appeal', by collecting specific food items (lentils, split peas, sugar and wholewheat flour) for Ethiopia, Somalia and the Sudan. As the crisis in Africa had developed, the school was already projecting its charity further afield – in November 1984 Dollis children were collecting postage stamps for the Blue Peter Appeal for Ethiopia, while their mothers were taking part in a 'knit-in' to make blankets for the same stricken nation. This much wider perspective on the charitable giving of the harvest assembly was to continue. Eleven years later the food gifts were being sent to needy families in Eastern Europe.

Mr Heasman was very keen to make the children, 'not only increasingly book conscious, but also lovers of books', and took the opportunity of the National Childrens' Book Week (30 September to 7 October 1978) to make, 'an immediate start'. A Red House Puffin Book Club was set up at Dollis, a new non-profit venture for the school which allowed children to order their own books via the club. It was, he noted, 'a painless way' to have a school bookshop. In March 1979 Mrs Olwen Pruski started a Puffin Club (promoted by Penguin Books), a similarly named but quite separate enterprise, in which she and her 'Puffineers' took part in events and outings of a literary nature, including a visit to the annual Puffin Club exhibition in London. And as these new clubs began, so too was work underway, with parental help, on a new fiction library for the school, to be created in the 'waiting space' corner of the entrance lobby, adjacent to what was then the school secretary's office – this space was then being used to display school photographs, and would subsequently (in 1992), be enclosed and made into the current school office. In March 1979 a reading bay (created in the space off the hall corridor, outside the medical room) was ready, complete with display boards, shelving, and electrical sockets for cassette players and headphones, to help the less able readers – subsequently this space became the school museum. In May 1979 the new fiction library was finished too, and that month a 'Buy-a-Book' fundraising campaign was started to boost the library's resources – by June a total of £591.23 had been collected, enabling the purchase of 300 new fiction books.

Once the new fiction library was carpeted in June (the floors were then tiled), attention turned to the next phase: the development of a central reference library which, with the help of the School Library Service, several teachers, and the Jeffrey family, was made ready for use (in one of the huts between the second and third-year corridors) by early November 1979. In February 1981 a separate Puffin Paperback library was given its own Puffin corner. Two book events, in 1982 and 1983, continued the headteacher's promotion of books and reading. Both featured special displays and activities, bookshops, and story telling by visiting authors. Book Event '83 was opened by Roald Dahl. Special book exhibitions in the school hall followed in 1984 and 1985. In June 1983 Dollis acquired its own book agent's licence from the Publishers' Association, enabling the school to operate its own bookshop, which then took the place of the Red House Puffin Book Club. Another, even more ambitious library scheme was undertaken in 1985: the conversion of two cloakrooms in the main cross-corridor, into a new central library which would house in one place both the school's reference collection and its fiction books. Money from the 1984 Summer Fête, and parental assistance in the form of voluntary labour, brought this major project to a successful conclusion by October 1985. The area once occupied by the fiction library was subsequently converted into the current school office, and the hut formerly occupied by the central reference library, became the language resources room (used for remedial reading), later still the school museum (1996), until again reverting to a classroom.

FIRST-HAND EXPERIENCES

The new headteacher had a strong belief that first-hand experiences should be at the centre of junior-school education, from meeting real authors face to face, to educational visits and school journeys which explored the local community, and beyond. If such things were not new in themselves, they were now given an entirely new emphasis, becoming prominent features of Dollis life. School journeys were given a strong personal endorsement by the headteacher, who made a point of visiting the parties that were on a school journey. In May 1979 Mr Heasman visited parties on the Isle of Wight and at Swanage. In May 1981 he was back on the Isle of Wight, a year later he was visiting a Dollis party at Boggle Hole, North Yorkshire. In the past school journeys had only been made by the older children, the parties made up from several classes, with not everyone being included. Now the goal was to get all of the classes out, right across the school. Mrs Pruski led the way for the younger children, taking her second-year class overnight to Ivinghoe in 1980, and her first-year class to same spot the next year (1981), staying at the youth hostel and spending time studying the village. In 1981 the advantages of using hired minibuses were noted when Mrs Shurmer's fourth-year class went to Barnard Castle. Mr Markwell and Mr Heasman accompanied the party, as did Mrs Heasman, who nobly prepared the meals at the youth hostels. To make the most of the school journeys, they were frequently followed up by presentations for parents and children, which could include both slides and tape recordings. In time all classes began to take part; in 1983, nine did so, the following year eleven classes out of twelve made a school journey. In 1986 the school acquired its own minibus, soon followed the next year by another.

The number of educational visits increased too, again much encouraged by Mr Heasman, not least by the example of Mr and Mrs Heasman together taking out groups of children. In 1982 they made two visits to the new Barbican Centre in London. The following year, in March, another lucky group was taken to Zoomballomballastic at the Poetry Society. In April a group of twenty went to the Royal Festival Hall for a concert, and in November the Heasmans were leading a walk in the Chilterns. Exploring the immediate local environment, in its broadest sense, from buildings to wildlife, was given a special boost by the headteacher in 1985 with the first of his 'out and about' excursions, taking classes on short note taking visits to local spots, something akin to the work done on the much longer school journeys. In conjunction with Dollis Infant School, a nature reserve was opened in 1983 on the school's own doorstep, in the area of the disused railway line.

Evening talks of an educational nature were arranged for parents. In April 1979 there was a talk and hall display on 'Science in the Junior School'; in November 1982 there was a 'Dollis Environmental Evening' all about Mill Hill; in September 1983 there was an evening on micro-computers. The appearance in the school of special visitors invited to talk to the children, became an ever more frequent occurrence. In March 1981 James Blades, the international percussion player, spent an afternoon at Dollis, the first of a long line of prominent personalities who were to come to the school over the next two decades. From September 1987 such visits became a regular programme of weekly 'Monday Morning' visitors, interviewed by the headteacher in the school hall in front of the whole school, with further questions from the children. There were special events, too: the book events of 1982 and 1983, but also others – a 'Mini-Arts Festival' in March 1984 – all precedents for the wide range of events held subsequently.

Mr Heasman was also a strong supporter of school dinners and healthy eating. He was surprised at the great number of children at Dollis who ate packed lunches, and he immediately set out to promote, and to improve, the school meals. They were 'excellent value for 25p', and very quickly, in October 1978, a choice of menu was introduced, together with a new 'continuous service' (from the end of that September) which cut the time the children spent waiting in the dining hall. The latter was so successful that by November it was possible to shorten the lunch break by fifteen minutes, which allowed afternoon school to begin at 1.10 p.m. instead of 1.25 p.m., which in turn meant that the children could go home earlier, at 3.45 p.m., instead of 4.00 p.m. To further promote a healthy diet an 'apple stall', run by the senior year children, was set up during the morning and afternoon breaks. Making its first appearance during the summer term of 1983, the idea subsequently grew to encompass a greater range of fruits, sold throughout the school year. To apples were added clementines, oranges, bananas and pineapple. Nor did the cost suffer from the inflation which has ever pushed up the price of school meals. Apples were 8p in 1983, but still only 10p in 1998. Other special promotions have included a remarkable number of hot-cross buns, such as were sold by year-six children in April 1997 – 1,500 in only four fifteen-minute breaks!

NEW WAYS AND OLD WAYS

The first years under Mr Heasman saw a gradual change in the staffing structure and organisation of the school. Whereas previously a teacher's scale had been simply according to the year they taught, it was now adjusted to take account of particular curriculum responsibilities. Teaching methods were changed, the old syllabuses were set aside and a great many old text books, and other dated resources, were thrown out.

Mrs Graham, the girls' needlework mistress had retired at the end of the 1977/78 year, and she was not replaced. Nor were the handwork lessons for boys continued: together with the girls' needlework classes they were replaced by 'a design and make scheme'. The French courses begun by Mr Patterson disappeared from the curriculum – indeed there was some concern among secondary school language teachers that such courses in primary schools were not always beneficial. This latter was the case with those secondary schools to which Dollis was a feeder – but the junior school did continue to offer some opportunity for French instruction in the form of a lunch-time French club, made available when a suitable teacher was on the staff. The new headteacher also turned his attention to the weekly radio broadcasts for schools, and in his own words, 'disconnected the contraption in my cupboard, which relayed the BBC weekly service to schools to every classroom'. However much the children might have enjoyed the Friday morning 'goody-goodies', they were abolished as being too 'competitive', with teachers spending too much class time on preparing them.

The school moved from a 'traditional' fixed timetable, in which every child did one hour each of maths, spelling and English every day, with regular weekly lessons in geography, history, nature, art and needlework or handwork, to a more open timetable where only music, games and the daily morning hall assemblies were held according to a fixed schedule. Previously it had been 'bells, clocks and periods', with the children literally changing subjects at the sounding of a bell. The headteacher could peruse the schedule, and know exactly what every class was doing at any particular time. Now, however, it was up to each Dollis teacher to devise their own schedule, a system that was supposed to allow greater opportunity for 'real education', enabling planning to be more 'open ended', allowing lessons to develop their own 'centre of interest', but without the teacher forcing it. Once a teacher and children became 'hooked' on a theme, they were to, 'feel completely free to develop it in every direction, inter relating all aspects of the curriculum' – though alongside this the headteacher still expected them to 'keep hammering home daily maths, spelling teaching, number bonds, good old fashioned mental arithmetic, teaching of grammar and handwriting'. Where teachers felt their children had earned it, they could be taken outside (in fine weather) for a quick ten minutes of organised rounders.

Apart from maths and reading, which were to be taught daily, teachers were free to decide how much or how little of a particular subject would be done in any given week – though they were initially (from September 1979) to prepare half-term predictions, covering all aspects of the curriculum, and were to submit each week a record of what had actually been done. From September 1983 the headteacher wanted every child to write at least one poem or story each week, a record of which was to be submitted by the class teacher every Monday morning, explaining how a particular piece of writing came about, and what points of English arose from it. Spelling, grammar and writing skills were to come out of the sessions spent on creative writing. Handwriting was given a special push for first and second-year classes during the last half of the summer term.

Teachers might be allowed greater flexibility but they had now to be certain that, 'records are carefully checked and a constant watch kept to see that all areas of the curriculum are taught'. This was where the danger lay – that work programmes would not be 'sufficiently structured and clear' and that the 'progression' of children over the course of a year, and from their first to their final year would not be properly monitored. It was an opportunity for the individual teacher, but also one which carried a greater responsibility. The setting up of individual children's records, to include details of any problems, interviews with parents etc, and specimens of work, to be handed on from class to class, became a matter of great importance.

The first years of the new headship witnessed many changes. Much of the old etiquette and remaining formalities that had long been a part of classroom life were further dissolved. The new headteacher no longer insisted that all stand whenever he entered, nor was there a formal greeting from the children – he now preferred them to simply keep working, while he had a quiet word with their teacher. From July 1979 the old 'Scholar's Report Book' was discontinued, and the first children went home with a new single-sheet report which allowed greater space for remarks by teachers under a series of more general headings: language and literacy, mathematics, environmental studies, creative skills, music, physical education and games, and personal development. It concluded with a summary and recommendations. From the beginning of the spring term, 1982, short trousers for boys (apart from those in their PE kit) were no longer insisted upon as part of the school uniform. From January 1984 tables and tray units began to replace the old desks (the inkwells of which had become an appendage of the past, used only as a receptacle for pencil shavings!).

More importantly, the hitting of children by class teachers – a slap on the legs or across the bottom – soon became a thing of the past, though the use of 'slippering' by the headteacher at Dollis remained, though very rarely used – up to a half dozen whacks in 1984 for the worst cases at Dollis, but always after Mr Heasman had the permission of parents. All corporal punishment came to an end in 1986, though certainly not all headteachers were in agreement. The Borough of Barnet's regulations on corporal punishment, set out in 1966, had been reviewed in 1972, and had been left without amendment. They were clear that corporal punishment, 'should never be severe and should be used only if it appears that other disciplinary measures are inappropriate and after due regard has been had to the emotional and psychological effects of the punishment on the individual child.' Such immediate chastisement as the boxing of ears, blows to the head or rapping the knuckles, were 'strictly prohibited.' The headteacher (though he might authorise its infliction by another teacher) was alone responsible for the use of corporal punishment, which, 'should only be inflicted with a cane.' Such punishment for girls was to be used only in the most 'exceptional circumstances', and then only on the hands.

In 1982 corporal punishment in the borough was again the subject of review, and in March 1983 the governing body for the schools of group XI, to which Dollis Junior School belonged, were told by the group's headteachers that there had been no cases of formal corporal punishment 'for some years'. The headteachers were, however, 'in agreement that they did not want the deterrent of the cane removed.' The group's governing body voted 6:2 to retain the 1966 regulations. Local views, however, were soon superseded by those expressed at Westminster, and in 1986 corporal punishment in schools was abolished.

In September 1989, to conform with the attempt to create a uniform national system, the designation of Dollis' classes as years one to four was changed to years three to six.

COMPUTING POWER!

As the older ways of order, discipline and punishment disappeared, a new technology, destined to have an enormous impact on schools, was making its first appearance: computers! When thoughts had turned to the possibility of a Summer Fête in 1982, one of the aims had been the purchase of a computer. Plans for the fête were dropped, but the following year (1983) Dollis became one of the first primary schools in Barnet to be given a computer by the Department of Industry & Trade – a BBC 'B' micro-computer, 'with disc interface 1.2 operating system with 100k disc drive and colour monitor'. This very first computer was moved around the school from class to class, enabling each to have access for a week at a time. It was then the Government's intention that every primary school should, eventually, have one such computer – but at Dollis the goal soon became one for every classroom, and the school soon got busy raising funds for 'computer resources' and a further micro-computer. Through some imaginative schemes (sponsored 'matchbox filling' and another 'Dollis Special' to York in October 1983), together with the now annual Christmas Bazaar and the traditional sponsored swim, the school soon had three such computers placed in the classroom corridors of the main building. On 7 December 1983 the school took delivery of its third BBC 'B' micro, a direct result of that year's Christmas Bazaar. A fourth computer (at a cost of £742, 'with all accessories') was placed on order as a direct result of the school's first regular Summer Fête of 1984.

This of course was only the beginning, for not only would more computers and more software be needed in the future, but they would soon need replacing by what was newer and better. Voucher schemes by such national firms as Tesco were to prove invaluable to Dollis in acquiring further computers in the early 1990s, but the school had always to look to its own initiatives as well. Typically, March of 1996 found the school on the tramp in a sponsored walk to raise money towards purchasing new IBM based computers for years three and four, to get them on a par with years five and six. The following year Dollis was able to shed its 'outgrown' computers, passing them on to Llanarmon County Primary School in Llangollen – a Dollis connection through Miss J. Thomas, whose mother was Llanarmon's headteacher. In 2000 Dollis opened its own computer suite, and in 2002 installed its first computer linked interactive electronic whiteboard.

DIFFICULT TIMES

During his very first year at Dollis Mr Heasman had faced a school caretakers' strike which threatened to close the school in the depths of winter. Over a period of six days (in January and February 1979) the new headteacher and his wife (temporarily serving as welfare assistant at Dollis), had to wrestle with frozen padlocks as they opened up the school in the mornings and closed it in the evenings. In his second year Mr Heasman had fallen ill, and was away from the school for much of the year (from the end of November 1979 to July 1980), during which time his duties were taken on by the deputy headteacher, Mr Peter Joy (whose class was then taken by a supply teacher). Nonetheless, in September 1983 Mr Heasman could look back at his first five years at Dollis with a sense of satisfaction. He had brought a new energy to the school and made many positive changes. As Dollis progressed into the mid-1980s, however, it came upon troubled times.

In common with other schools, there was much disruption caused by the teachers' 'Industrial Action' of 1984-86. Against the background of a bitter national strike by coal miners, the teachers resorted to strike action themselves, over pay and conditions. From the 1 May 1984 there was recurring and prolonged disruption, which was to continue for the next two years, until the spring of 1986. At Dollis classes had to be cancelled and children sent home, often on very short notice, the result of 'no cover' action by the school's NUT (National Union of Teachers) members. Lunchtime clubs and after-school activities were suspended as were staff meetings and teacher/parent consultations. The Dollis children missed out on two district sports meetings and swimming galas, in 1984 and 1985. For Mr Heasman, who unlike his predecessor did not himself take part in any of the strike actions, it was a particularly stressful time as he strove to keep the school open with as little disruption as could be managed. But with union members working to the letter of their contracts (and at Dollis the 'action' was 'fully implemented in every detail'), there was inevitably discord, and an extremely trying and fretful time was experienced by all who were caught up in it.

As the striking teachers refused to do lunchtime duty, the headteacher had regularly to do it himself, undertaking it largely unaided, save for the assistance of his deputy. In addition the headteacher found himself on occasion having to take charge of two, three or even four classes of children at a time, to cover for missing teachers. As the school's football coach would not enter the Dollis team on account of the 'Action', Mr Heasman stepped in himself, taking the boys to a series of friendlies. In the summer term (1985), having been twice advised to take time off because of persistent and severe headaches attributed to stress, he finally succumbed, taking work home, and coming in and out of school as needed.

As the strike worsened through 1985, Mr Heasman was relaying to the borough's education officers, by letter and by telephone call, all the minutiae of every 'unreasonable' act committed by the school's union members – and anxiously awaiting their response. In the autumn term there was a row over the refusal of certain teachers to use portable gas heaters provided by the borough. The chairman of the school governors was called in as a witness, and the borough's education office was fully informed as to which teachers thought the heaters were too dangerous, and which felt they were simply too smelly! In December, with thoughts turning to Christmas, the headteacher was requesting the advice of the borough's education office over the refusal of union members to contribute to a Christmas display in the school hall! The chief education officer, if nonplussed, was faultlessly polite – it was 'of course regrettable', but he did not think 'there was very much we can do about it'! The 'Action' continued unabated, and in January (1986) the headteacher was again at home, unwell and needing a rest.

Headteachers could be put under immense strain, as Mr Heasman made clear in his reports to the school's governors. He also included the school secretary and the welfare assistant among those particularly affected by the strike action. No mention, however, was made of the deputy headteacher, though it would appear that those who served in this role found their situation an exceptionally stressful one – over the course of the strikes, from May 1984 to the spring of 1986, there were no less than five different deputy, or acting deputy, headteachers.

Mr Peter Joy, Heasman's first deputy, had left Dollis in December 1980, after more than eight years at the school, and having twice served as the acting headteacher, the last time for most of the 1979/80 year. The school governors were unanimous in commending 'the efficient way he carried out his duties' during Mr Heasman's prolonged illness, a feeling shared by parents. Mr Joy's replacement, Trevor Bartlett, who had arrived in April 1981, was still in place when the strike action began, but in December 1984 he left to take up a headship of his own. Replacing him proved to be very difficult. Maurice Markwell (teaching at Dollis since September 1980) was called upon to fill in as an acting deputy, and did so until the appointment of Mr Jim Betts in April 1985. Betts's arrival coincided with a time of considerable stress for the headteacher. When the headteacher finally took time off, his new deputy was left to cope with the school's problems on his own. On one occasion he was physically threatened by another teacher. By the close of the term he had resigned, having found his position, 'too stressful'. That autumn Barnet's chief education officer was expressing concern over Betts's resignation and 'the reluctance of the senior members of staff to take on the duties of acting deputy head', all of which seemed to indicate 'a certain tension' at Dollis, further exacerbated by the ongoing 'Industrial Action'. Miss Oddy, the school's music teacher, who had in fact been on a deputy headship course and would subsequently become a headteacher herself, expressed her dislike of a 'management style' at the school which she felt threw far too great a burden onto the shoulders of the school's deputy headteacher.

In the short term the problem of the deputy headship was resolved by the appointment of another acting deputy headteacher, Mrs Christine Taylor. Finally, in April 1986, Mr Graham Lancaster was appointed as the Dollis deputy headteacher. In the spring too, the NUT finally relented, announcing that, 'there would be a return to peace and calm in schools'. Over the period of the strikes Dollis had been, 'badly effected … staff meetings, reports, meetings with parents, [and] records largely shelved'. At the start of the new autumn term of 1986, a quarter of the teaching staff were newcomers.

DANTE'S INFERNO?

During the teachers' 'Action', the difficulties experienced at Dollis had been made far worse by the very unwelcome reappearance of an all too familiar Dollis problem, a breakdown of the heating system, which now required a complete overhaul. Moreover, yet again, this coincided with the always timely arrival of the authority's decorators! It was hardly surprising that the headteacher had been affected by stress!

Dollis heating problems were already of long standing and went back to the earliest years of the school's existence. Mr Heasman was made all too aware of them during his very first winter in the school. He soon realised that he had inherited a boiler system which was 'somewhat useless when the cold is severe'. That February (1979) the headteacher brought his own electric convector heater into school and invited other teachers to do the same. It was little enough, but new boilers were soon delivered. If, however, anyone thought that some solution had been achieved, they were all too soon disabused of the notion. In February 1983 the school's two boilers were again behaving erratically, causing a drop in temperature which resulted in a morning's extended hymn singing in the school hall – where the DES's tolerable temperatures for schools had a lower threshold than in classrooms. A year later the three classrooms in the fourth (senior)-year corridor had to be closed for a month while the floors were ripped up and faulty heating pipes – now thirty-two years old and buried in concrete – were replaced. The reference library, the fiction library, the dining area and the music room were used as alternative classrooms, while the music teacher, Miss Oddy, operated from, 'a cupboard in the third year corridor'. This, however, was but a prelude to the troubles which started on 8 February 1985 when another old and rusted pipe sprang a leak under the floor of the fiction library. A repair was soon effected but the school had to be closed for two days. Barnet's senior heating engineer gave a grim, and all too prophetic, warning, which by the end of the month had come true in the form of yet another major leak, this time in the administrative corridor. In the meantime the heating in the HORSA classrooms had also failed, necessitating a move for both of the resident junior (first year) classes. But there was more to come: on 5 March an even worse leak erupted between the hall and the main corridor, and true to Dollis's past history, a team of decorators had turned up the previous day with bucket, brush and roller, to start work on the classrooms! They soon had their own problems as their paint at first failed to adhere! Not to be left out, a lorry load of new school furniture arrived on the same day – new tables, chairs and storage units, all looking for a home! Classes were again on the move, to the ear-rattling clatter of pneumatic drills biting into concrete. Where the engineers were working steam was 'issuing forth out of the hot pipes, the area … a cross between Roman Baths and roadworks on the M1'. The heating engineers and the decorators were soon joined by carpenters sent to the school with orders to make repairs in the music room, (itself then in use as a temporary classroom), and by an electrician trying to re-route a mains cable which had always been next to the heating pipes. There were absences from the teaching staff – three on one day, which left seventy-five children without a teacher until they were parcelled out to other classes – and all this against the background of the continuing strike action by the school's NUT members. Not surprisingly the headteacher came to see it as the 'most trying and stressful' year he had ever experienced, the school 'being rocked by one incident after another'.

Dollis made the front page of the local press. The next day the headteacher announced that he had received word from the town hall that the school's heating pipes were to be completely replaced – something he had been requesting, without effect, for several years! This time they were to be placed along the top of the walls, not buried in concrete under the floor, but the promised renewal did not take place that summer – instead it began in the middle of the following autumn term. The heating contractors commenced work on 28 November 1985. Once again classes were on the move, and once more children had their lessons against a background noise of drilling and banging, as heating engineers and builders became a part of Dollis life for the third winter running. The work continued into the spring term, its completion delayed when in February the newly installed system suffered its first breakdown – made good by bringing in calor-gas heaters, a situation rather reminiscent of the efforts to keep Dollis's first occupants warm in the unfinished school, during the winter of 1951/52. If this was not all depressing enough, that same February of 1986 the school became a victim of arson – a fire set by three of its own pupils! Fortunately the damage was confined to one classroom only.

STAFF AND CLASSES

From the high point reached in the autumn of 1970, there was a gradual decline in the number of children on the Dollis Junior School roll. In January 1981 it was down to 323 children, and thereafter the numbers declined more sharply – as in fact had been predicted. In 1983 they fell below 300 (to 282) and in 1984 reached a record low of 269. In Mr Heasman's first year there were twelve classes at Dollis – nine in the main school building, two in the HORSA hut and one in the huts set between the finger corridors, which left a spare hut there, which in 1979 became the central reference library (and later the language resources room, and later still the school museum). Apart from a thirteenth class which appeared for one year (1979/80) the school maintained twelve classes from September 1978 to July 1993. From the record low figure reached in 1984, the number of children rose gradually, to settle around the 300 mark by the end of the 1980s. In the 1990s, however, quite in line with predictions, the number of school children began to increase significantly. In 1992/93 there were 360 children distributed among the twelve classes. For September 1993 it was decided to create a thirteenth class, and from September 1995 an extra class was added each year for the next three years, the roll having climbed to 399 in January 1996, to 422 a year later and up to 451 by January 1998, by which time (from September 1997) there were sixteen classes. To support this, the one time 'spare hut' reverted to being a classroom, while in 1994 three new classrooms were built onto the year-six corridor, being ready for use early in 1995. In 1993 the two HORSA classrooms (occupied by juniors since 1948) were passed over to the infant school, the juniors so displaced taking up residence in a mobile double hut received in January of that year from Ravenscroft School. The number of junior classes remained fixed at sixteen but the junior school's intake continued to climb, boosted further by its growing popularity. The roll had reached 472 by January 2000, 485 a year later and 505 by January 2002.

The number of school staff also expanded in the 1990s. For September 1995 the headteacher had under his direction a deputy headteacher, and fourteen full-time class teachers, to which were added a part-time teaching staff of two music teachers, one special educational needs co-ordinator and six support teachers (including one for 'learning' and another for 'languages') – making twenty-five teachers (including the headteacher) in all. There were in addition four teachers' assistants. The support staff consisted of one administrator, one administrative assistant, one part-time word processor operator, a welfare officer, a site manager and three cleaners. There was one senior meal-time supervisor, with five supervisors (of whom two were also teachers' assistants) under her. The site manager also stood in as the school crossing patrol. In all there were forty-one staff members, with a further five kitchen staff (one cook and four assistants). By way of contrast, when Mr Heasman had started at Dollis there were, besides himself, fourteen teachers, of whom twelve were class teachers, one a music and French teacher, and one a remedial teacher. The support staff had consisted of a welfare assistant, a secretary (or clerical assistance), a caretaker, and an assistant caretaker (who were shared with the infant school), a school crossing patrol, and four 'dinner ladies' who helped with the lunchtime supervision – making a total of twenty-four staff. In addition the kitchen had a cook and four general assistants.

Over time the school's internal management structure also changed. In 1978 there had been simply the headteacher and his deputy (who also had a class), with a senior mistress (girls) and a senior master (boys). Ten years later this had been changed, the school's hierarchy running from headteacher to deputy headteacher, and down to four 'year leaders', one for each of the school's year groups. From September 1996 a further change was made to this structure by the insertion of two 'senior teachers' (then a relatively new appointment) above the year leaders, one to be head of the lower school (years three and four) and the other to be head of the upper school (years five and six). That year too, the children themselves were given a means to make a contribution to 'the whole school decision making process'. A school council, consisting of two elected pupil representatives from each class, met with the deputy headteacher for the first time in May 1996. In 1997 the council requested a school 'Mufti Day', when children could come to school out of uniform, paying 50p each for the privilege, the money being put towards the development of the playgrounds. In 1998 seven of the pupil representatives from the council were elected by their fellows to participate in the planning of the 'No Bullies Here!' week, intended for that October.

FROM MANAGERS TO GRANT MAINTAINED

In 1980 the school's managers were transformed into governors, as the managing bodies of primary schools became governing bodies. Dollis, whether 'managed' or 'governed', was still one of a group of four schools – the others being the Dollis Infant School, The Fairway JMI and the Courtland JMI. The governing body's vice-chairman was Councillor Sorrell, who happened also to be a Dollis parent. Meetings were held termly. That of July 1981, held at Dollis, was typical. Eight governors, and two officials from the town hall were present, and the headteachers of the four schools were also in attendance. After a walk around the school, the meeting proper began at 6.15 p.m., and proceeded with the due formalities. For the first hour all were present, as matters pertaining to all four schools were discussed, but thereafter membership became more selective. At 7.15 p.m. Miss Hall, then headteacher of the Dollis Infant School, prepared to deliver her annual report to the governors – at which point the other three headteachers were required to leave the school hall, where the meeting was taking place. When Miss Hall had finished, and after any matters arising had been discussed, Mr Heasman was then invited in, and Miss Hall shown out, as the Dollis Junior School headteacher was now to give his own report. The meeting closed at 8.30 p.m., with the governors expressing their interest in what was happening at the junior school, especially the new emphasis on school journeys.

Over the next years the governing body did begin to see real change. In 1982, in line with the local education committee's desire to encourage parental representation, the governing body of Dollis's group of schools increased the number of parent governors from one to two – but these two governorships were to be shared among the four schools. Moreover they were also co-optative governors, appointed by the body's representative governors. From September 1985 each school (or pair of schools on the same site, as in the case of Dollis Junior School and Dollis Infant School) was to have its own governing body, and there was to be one parent and one teacher on each governing body. The parent governor was to be elected by the parents of the children. The first Dollis Junior School parent governor so elected was Alan Rockall, while the first teacher governor was Maurice Markwell. At the same time headteachers also became governors.

Formal parental representation on the governing body was increased again from the autumn of 1988, with the inclusion of two parent governors for each of the Dollis schools, and could be added to further by the inclusion of parents among the co-opted governors – as indeed there could be parents among the appointed governors as well. In November the readers of *School News* were given the details of the new governing body for the two Dollis schools. In total there were seventeen governors: four governors appointed by the LEA (local education authority), two parent governors elected for each of the schools, two teacher governors (one from each school), the two headteachers themselves, and another five co-opted governors. Significantly the latter included the local beat constable, Peter Petts, and Major Patricia Ridley-Jones, representing Inglis Barracks.

For the junior school further change of even greater significance was just in the offing. In 1988 the school was invited to become one of the eight Barnet schools piloting the Government's new LMS (local management of schools) scheme. From April 1989, Dollis Junior School received a delegated budget of £300,000, a new situation which necessitated the creation of a governors' finance sub-committee – previously the headteacher had control of an allotment of only £6,000. The advantages of LMS were quickly apparent. A measure of financial independence freed the school from at least some of the bureaucracy and red tape attached to even a simple repair, such as getting a broken classroom window re-glazed. By contrast the local authority's changes to the way schools were to be cleaned, was concurrently producing much disquiet, and not a few untidy classrooms. The headteacher was soon suggesting that the Government's new grant-maintained status (GMS) for schools might offer even better value for money. In May 1990 copies of the Government's booklet on GMS were sent out to all Dollis Junior School parents. It was the beginning of a long campaign which led finally to a ballot of parents in February/March 1993. The final result was a vote in favour of grant-maintained status, though it was not an overwhelming endorsement, despite a great deal of effort to provide parents with information, and to persuade them. Only 64 per cent of the eligible parents voted, of whom 186 were in favour, and 159 against the proposed change. Nevertheless it was enough, and the school's application for grant maintained status was approved, and from 1 September 1993, Dollis Junior School became a grant-maintained school.

It was undoubtedly a landmark in the school's history. At last the school acquired its own governing body, and with it complete control over its own budget. Its new found independence laid the foundation for further improvements to both buildings and resources, and much improved levels of staffing. One early result of the school's new GM status was the securing of a grant to build three new classrooms on to the year-six corridor. The work began in April 1994 and was finished by the following January. Additionally the school was able to appoint its own cleaners, once the contract arranged by Barnet ran out at the end of July 1994. It led to an immediate improvement.

Having achieved GM status (in reality a further extension of the LMS status acquired in 1989) the school left behind some of the more … trying … aspects of local authority control which had long been part of school life. No longer would the school have to suffer from the unsolicited, and often untimely, arrival of decorators, window cleaners, and other contractors. No more would there be queries from the audit section over the marks appearing in the dinner register, or difficulties over the authority's rules for providing 'cover' for absent teachers. No longer would word be received 'from the Town Hall' that the headteacher was, 'to take immediate steps to record *Daily* readings of electricity, gas meters and oil gauges' in conjunction with his caretaker (November 1979). Nor would the headteacher be required to explain why the school telephone had recently seen unusually high use (June 1982)! The school telephone seems to have been a bit of a sore point. Private calls were to be avoided, and official ones were to be 'as brief as possible'. Headteachers were asked 'to impose a restriction' on all calls between 9 a.m. and 1 p.m. to avoid the higher rate band. In March 1982 headteachers were 'reminded' that no long-distance calls were to be made on the school telephone, 'unless it is a matter of *extreme emergency*' … and then such calls should *only* be made *after* 1 p.m.! Should teachers be called upon to do jury service, they were to be certain to submit form 5223 before attending court, as this enabled the local authority to deduct an amount from that teacher's pay equal to the jury service allowance. Should a teacher be sick during the summer holiday, he or she was to, 'advise the Teachers Section, Friern Barnet Town Hall of the date when they became unfit and the date when they would have been fit to work' – a ruling which applied to both teachers and to non teaching monthly paid staff in all the authority's schools (July 1984).

SOME SPORTING NOTABLES

The new headteacher of 1978 was a strong supporter of school sports, a successful school football coach himself and a keen cricket enthusiast. Rounders was soon introduced as an inter-house sport, with Nicoll being the first winner of the Dollis Rounders Shield. In 1981 cricket made an appearance. Fourth-year boys were given instruction by Jack Robertson, former Middlesex and England opening batsman. In 1983 all of the third year boys were receiving instruction from a qualified MCC cricket coach. Always on the look out for new sports to add to the school's curriculum, a 'short tennis' set was purchased in 1985, following a demonstration given to the first-year children.

The school's sporting prowess was on prominent display in the early 1980s. The Dollis swimmers won the West Barnet District Swimming Shield in 1980, 1981 and 1982, and again in 1986. In 1982 the school's swimming relay teams (the boys' team and the girls' team) won their respective trophies at the Middlesex Championships. Girls' netball had resumed at Dollis in October 1978, and under the enthusiastic guidance of Mrs Mountford the team won the West Barnet Primary Schools Shield with a convincing performance in 1981 and again in 1982 – the first time the shield had been won in consecutive years. March of 1981 saw an extraordinary finals match in the Barnet Primary Schools Badminton Tournament. Both girls' pairs from Dollis reached the finals, and played each other for the trophy!

After many years without any great success, the football team won the league trophy cup in 1981. Further notable success proved elusive for some time, but in 1991-92 Dollis again enjoyed an outstanding season, achieving a Barnet Schools' West Region double, the league title and the Martin Cup, and reaching the semi final of the Middlesex competition, the Alf Gant Cup. The next two seasons saw the team win the West Barnet League title twice more, making a run of three years. In 1992-93 they shared the Martin Cup with St Joseph's after a hard fought final, and the following year, though they lost to Broadfields in the Martin Cup final, they beat the same team only weeks later, to win the League Champions Cup Final. Two years later the team of 1994-95 progressed as far as the final of the prestigious all London Black Cup, but lost to Lavendar School after an exciting and exhausting match. But the best was yet to come – in March 1998 Dollis's footballers were again in the Black Cup final, and to the delight of the four coach loads of supporters who turned out to cheer Dollis on, the boys did it! They beat Whybridge Junior School 2 to 1 and took the cup! The headteacher declared it to be, 'one of the greatest achievements and days in the forty-six year history of the school'.

In 1995 Dollis Junior School became the first school in Barnet to start a judo club. Two years later the school's judo club members took home an impressive haul of medals from the first London Primary School Championships – eight gold, nine silver and ten bronze. The local press dubbed them 'Dynamite Dollis', the 'toast of London.' It was an excellent beginning for what has proved to be a popular after-school club.

FINAL STROKES: THE POOL

Swimming remained an integral part of the school curriculum, with swimming certificates being given out regularly in assembly. In 1981 some 150 were awarded. The school's own learner pool continued to provide a useful facility, near at hand, but from the autumn of 1979 the fourth (senior) year children started having their weekly lessons at nearby Copthall Pool. In 1981 they were joined by the third-year children. At first the children were conveyed to Copthall Pool by a coach hired by the school (25p a head in September 1982), but in June 1984 such luxury came to an end, with teachers and children being told to walk, making use of the footpath opened in 1978 between the pool and Pursley Road. In June 1986 the inter-house swimming gala, until then 'a very low key event' held in the Dollis pool, went to a much grander venue at Copthall, and became a far more prominent school event – its first organisers were Mrs Taylor, Mrs Thomson and Mr Markwell.

The addition of a thermal cover, solar panels and improvements to the water heating system, kept the water in the school's learner pool warmer for longer. But the pool was still plagued by its old problems – breakdowns (a 'major breakdown' in September 1985) and vandals. In the spring of 1985 the pool came under assault from vandals who attempted to make holes in a costly new pool cover, jumped off the roof into the pool, broke down part of the fencing around the pool and used the area as an outdoor lavatory! They were reportedly as young as six and not much older than thirteen. Nonetheless the summer of 1986 found the pool 'going better than for many years', with the first-year children thoroughly enjoying their lessons. After the autumn of 1987 the pool lay idle, closed by another breakdown in its heating system, damage to the solar panels and finally by gales which destroyed the pool's wooden fencing. The cost of covering over the pool was prohibitive, as was its restoration. Vandalism continued to be a problem and by March 1992 it had been decided that the pool would not be re-opened – that August the pool was finally demolished. It was a fate shared with other such open-air pools across Barnet.

MAKING MUSIC

Dollis already had a well established musical tradition, which both Mr Paterson and his recorders, and especially Mr Sowerby, the school's music and French teacher from 1974, had done much to promote. With Mr Sowerby's departure at the end of December 1981 two Dollis musical traditions came to a close – the school's own annual Christmas carol concerts, and the school's participation in Christmas carol services at the Free church and at the Union church, both of which saw final performances in December 1981. But where old traditions came to an end, new ones took their place. From April 1982 Miss Michelle Oddy became the school's new music specialist. The evening carol concerts in the school hall, which had featured the choir and orchestra, were replaced by a new 'Christmas entertainment', which was 'a whole school effort' in which all children were to take part. The first one, in December 1982, was dubbed *Christmas Magic* and saw the children, arrayed in school uniform, put on three separate performances. The following year's production, *The Christmas Music Hall* featured an audience sing-along, with Victorian shops and children in costume. In December 1984 *The Big Red Book* took the stage. These were the first in what would become a long line of school 'productions', the task of organising and directing them falling to the school's music teacher.

Miss Oddy, Mr Sowerby's successor, was responsible for these early productions. Her position as 'music consultant', as described for 1984, required that she undertake two school productions, 'a two night stand' at the end of the autumn term and another 'musical evening/afternoon' during the summer term. She was to see that violin and cello lessons were continued, and was explicitly conjoined to see that recorder playing was developed and extended, 'that as many children who want to learn to play the recorder have the chance to do so.' She was to run the school orchestra and choirs, and to encourage the development of 'informal singing groups with guitar accompaniment'. The storage and maintenance of all musical equipment, and the keeping of an inventory of instruments, records and tape cassettes, fell to her, and she was also to be responsible for setting up the new resources room in the administrative corridor. She was to arrange for musicians to visit the school, and was expected occasionally to take groups of children to concerts. She was to provide guidance on television and radio music programmes, and to look into the possibility of introducing new musical instruments. It was at this time too that the music room was furnished and carpeted. Miss Oddy is remembered by former pupils for her conduct of Friday hymn singing, and some may also recall a winter's night in December 1982 when some 120 Dollis children, parents and teachers went carol singing. Miss Oddy arranged for the loan of an army lorry, with driver, 'into which one of the school pianos was hoisted, enabling the children to have piano accompaniment as they sung'. No money was collected, 'but much pleasure was given'.

In April 1986 the new deputy headteacher, Mr Graham Lancaster, took over a modified music timetable, and made the school's music room his base. Miss Oddy, now teaching a first-year class, left the following year, and subsequently secured a headship in Haringey. Under Mr Lancaster's direction the school continued to produce some notable whole-school Christmas productions – *Cinderella-Belle of the Ball* in 1987 and another Victorian-style *Christmas Music Hall* the following year. Plans for *Oliver*, the Christmas production for December 1989, were postponed when in November Mr Lancaster was knocked off his motorbike and seriously injured. It finally went on stage a year later in December 1990, together with a year-three production entitled *Christmas Gold*.

As the number of children at Dollis began to grow through the early 1990s, the idea of having *all* children take part in these productions was modified – the upper school (years five and six) and the lower school (years three and four) each put on their own productions. December 1991 saw *Aladdin* performed by the young thespians of years five and six under Mr Lancaster's direction, while Mrs Janet Watt headed up a team which produced Dollis's first lower-school production, *The Flight of the Bumblesnouts*. Subsequently the upper-school production usually occurred before Christmas, followed by that of the lower school in the spring term.

Mr Lancaster left the school in April 1992 for a headship at Livingstone School, East Barnet, his duties as music teacher being taken over temporarily by Miss E. Haffenden, and his mantel as production manager being taken up by Miss L. Ellis, who wrote and directed *Snow White* (December 1992) and *Jungle Book* the next year. In the meantime, from September 1993, Dollis had acquired two music specialists, Mr Colin Dowland and Miss Louise Spooner, each working at Dollis for half a week. With these appointments music was given renewed life. Even before taking up his appointment, Mr Dowland was writing in *School News* to encourage children to take up an instrument, and to further stimulate interest he appeared with the Barnet String Quartet to give a short concert. The children reciprocated with an 'overwhelming' response to Mr Dowland's offer of lessons, and in the autumn there was 'a tremendous surge' in the number of instrumental lessons being given, while additionally all of the year-three children were put to work learning the recorder under Miss Spooner. Singing too was given further stimulation, with Mr Dowland introducing 'The Singing Cup', a silver trophy to be awarded every half term to the class which made the best effort in Friday hymn practice and during class singing lessons. By June 1994 the school had thirty-one children learning the violin, sixteen the clarinet or the flute, another thirty-three strumming the guitar, with six more on the cello, seven on the drums, and eight on cornet or trumpet, while the school orchestra could boast forty-four members. That July the school had its first 'summer serenade', extended to two nights the following year.

The junior and senior choirs grew in strength (forty-five and fifty singers respectively by December 1994), and the now long-established tradition of school productions continued apace, with the upper school's *Wizard of Oz* (December 1994), followed by *A Christmas Carol* (1995), with *Charlie and the Chocolate Factory* the lower-school production of February 1996. The Christmas production of 1996 was an extravaganza by Mr Paul Tivey and Miss Seagrove, an adaptation of *The Lion, The Witch and the Wardrobe*, and was followed in the spring term by Mr Dowland's first 'cabaret' and a *Cinderella* production by years three and four. Another version of *Oliver* took to the Dollis stage in December 1997, again under the direction of Mr Tivey, with support from Mr Dowland and Miss Louise McCarthy. The following May (1998) the lower school put on *Alice*. That December there was no production – instead there was a special year-six 'Christmas Words and Music' evening. In the spring there was the now customary 'cabaret', followed by an intriguingly titled lower-school production, *Roald Dahl meets the Tudors*. The decade (and the millennium) was seen out by the appropriately titled *Moving On*, performed by years five and six in December 1999. The first of the 2000 productions fell to years three and four who, in June, put on a production which again featured the Bumblesnouts, in *The Bumblesnouts Save the World*.

It had been a part of the music consultant's brief in the 1980s to introduce new instruments to the school, but it was the Dollis children of the 1990s who were to be a part of Barnet school music 'history' when, in early 1995, Dollis Junior School became the first school in Barnet to have a steel band – a complete set of twelve pans sent from Trinidad. Interest in steel bands at Dollis had started with a visit in September 1994 from the steel band of the Aylward Comprehensive School in Edmonton. There was immediately enthusiasm for the idea of creating a Dollis band, and a target of £1,800 to purchase a set of steel pans was set for that year's Christmas Bazaar. A visit from Mr Terry Noel, a Trinidadian player, pushed the project on, with Mr Noel acting as Dollis agent in the acquisition of the pans. The Christmas Bazaar target was reached and a fine set of pans duly arrived in the new year. In January 1995 the Dollis children were in for a treat when for the first time the school hall boomed to the lilting melodies of the new Dollis pans, ably played by a teacher quintet composed of Mr Dowland, Miss Spooner, Miss Tuli, Miss Haffenden and Mr Tivey. Lessons started soon after, with groups of children receiving a series of three lessons, on a rota basis. All year groups were included, and by May the school had its own specialist teacher, Miss Rachel Hayward, national steel-pan soloist champion of 1989. That July (1995), at the summer serenade, an appreciative audience heard the children put on their first public performance on the pans.

By the autumn of 1996 Miss Hayward (herself the first british soloist to compete in Trinidad's steel-band competition) was planning to take her young players into the public limelight, entering them for competition, and also to have them play some 'gigs'. That fall the school's steel-pan players acquired a proper name, the Dollis Deep Pans, and the pans themselves a coat of bright yellow and green paint! The first public outings were a great success – they appeared on ITV's *London Today* programme that October, and over the next two years (1997 and 1998) won through to the prestigious National Festival of Music for Youth finals, held at the Royal Festival Hall, London. The Deep Pans soon had a 'pantastic'(!) reputation, their school performances always greeted with much enthusiastic applause. In June 1999 they took their talents abroad to Slovenia, at the request of the british ambassador. The trip was a great success – and a notable 'first' for Dollis.

Nor were the Deep Pans Dollis's only noteworthy music achievement at this time. In May 1996 Mr Dowland took the senior choir to the BBC studios in White City where they recorded ten 'Songs for School Assemblies', for release as a CD with accompanying book.

If however the Deep Pans were a great new success, that other 'traditional' school instrument, the recorder, was losing ground. In the mid-1990s all children during their first three years at Dollis were using recorders as part of their regular weekly music lesson, and as it was desirable that each child should have their own instrument, the school shop was selling recorders at £3 each. By the end of the 1990s, however, the recorder had become a matter of choice, and the number of players dwindled at one point to near extinction.

PUBLIC RECOGNITION

After six years at Dollis as deputy headteacher, Graham Lancaster had left in April 1992 to become the headteacher at Livingstone School, East Barnet. His replacement, from September 1992, was Mrs Carol Livingstone, then teaching service children at the Derby School in Osnabruck, Germany, an experience of advantage at Dollis, in view of the many children who still came from Inglis Barracks. Mrs Livingstone stayed for three years, and herself secured a headship at Deansbrook Junior School, leaving Dollis in December 1995. She was succeeded at Dollis by one of the headteacher's own sons, Matthew Heasman, who, arriving as an NQT (newly qualified teacher) in September 1989, had become a year leader in September 1991, an acting deputy headteacher seven months later (April-July 1992) and finally deputy headteacher in May 1996, having again served as acting deputy from January of that year.

The headteacher had been considering his own retirement at this very time (1995). The school was due to undergo its first OFSTED (Office for Standards in Education) inspection, an experience that was proving a stressful one for many headteachers. A letter of resignation was in fact written, but then withdrawn. The headteacher now had the close support of his own son as deputy headteacher, and when in June 1996 the OFSTED inspectors arrived, the inspection proved a great success. The inspectors found Dollis to be, 'very popular, well led and successful'. Its pupils made good progress and attained, 'sound or better standards in most areas of the curriculum'. It was, 'a very caring community which makes an outstanding contribution to pupils' personal development.' Its SATs results were 'good', and over the next years were to improve. The OFSTED inspection of 1996 was the first of a succession of public accolades which were to come to Dollis in the following years. That same year the school received an 'Investors in People Award', the first school in Barnet, Enfield and Haringey to do so. It was achieved only after a lengthy process begun at the end of 1994. In 1997, the school was the recipient of a Grant Maintained Schools Award of Excellence. Among other things, it was particularly commended for its music and drama, its school journey programme, the Monday visitors, the weekly *School News*, and the many physical improvements made to the main school building and its facilities over the preceding four years. In 1997 Dollis also received Barnet's Healthy Schools Initiative Award, the result of two years work led by senior teacher Mark Stubbings.

In 1999 Dollis was re-accredited as an Investor in People, the plaque being unveiled by Mr Chris Woodhead, HMCI (Her Majesty's Chief Inspector) – this was his second visit to Dollis, his first being in January 1996 when he unveiled a plaque commemorating the school becoming self-governing. In 2000 a 'short' inspection by OFSTED again commended the school highly, '… a very successful school … popular with parents and has a good reputation in the community which is well deserved … the school is excellently led by the Headteacher and senior staff.' The following year (2001) it received a School Achievement Award (for substantially improved results over the 1997-2000 period), was named as a Gold Star school in HMCI's annual report, and became a Beacon School. The achievements of the school were further recognised by awarding its headteacher an OBE. In 2002 the school was re-accredited again as an Investor in People, and in 2003 was awarded the Basic Skills Agency Quality Mark.

In February 2002, as part of Dollis Junior School's fiftieth birthday celebrations, there was an afternoon visit from HRH the Prince of Wales. The headteacher had extended a personal invitation to the prince, and was delighted by his acceptance. Mr Heasman described the visit as 'an incredible honour, an incredible privilege – a day of days'. It was, he said, the 'highlight' of his career, and in its aftermath he took the decision to finally retire, a resolution coinciding with the departure of his son Matthew, promoted to a headship of his own. It was a decision, which at a stroke, would leave the school without both a headteacher and a deputy headteacher! The academic year 2002/2003 would be Heasman's last as headteacher, though as it turned out, not his last at Dollis.

Mr Heasman could look back with a sense of achievement. Like his predecessors he had contributed much to the school, and had also seen it win special public recognition – but he was not destined to see out his final days as headteacher in peace and tranquillity! On 4 July 2003, with the end of his last term nearly at hand, a sudden power surge wreaked havoc at the school, knocking out telephones, computers, and copying equipment, and generally causing a degree of chaos. It was more than a week before the damaged cable under Pursley Road could be repaired, and all returned to normality. Perhaps in one way it was not such a bad way to remember Dollis – never a dull moment!

Ready to deliver harvest gifts, October 1978.

Commonwealth Day
assembly, March 1979.

Car accident, Pursley Road,
May 1979. (*Hendon Times*)

Miss Jane Mountford and
Dollis girls win the netball
shield, April 1981, and again
in 1982. (*Hendon Times*)

Mr Sowerby and the school orchestra, July 1981.

Dollis in bloom, results of the first hyacinth competition, February 1982. (*Hendon Times*)

Mrs Pruski, children, Councillor Sorrell (in minibus) and Mr Hale, ready to depart on a three-day school journey to Windsor, June 1982. (*Hendon Times*)

Above: Record breaking Dollis relay swimming teams with their trophy shields from the Middlesex Primary Schools' swimming championships, July 1982. (*Hendon Times*)

Right: Chaos at Dollis, burst pipes and teachers' strike, March 1985. Mrs Simons with pupils in the fiction library by the entrance lobby. (*Hendon Times*)

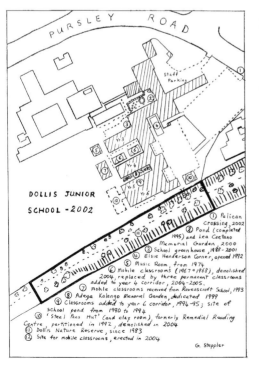

Above: Lunch is served! Open day, March 1988. Tom Shine, borough education officer, and Councillor Anthony Antoniou are in the queue.

Left: Dollis Junior School., 2002.

DOLLIS IN THE PRESENT

INTO THE TWENTY-FIRST CENTURY

INTRODUCTION

A school is an enterprise run by a particular headteacher, in a distinctive way. It is also a community which, over time, develops its own unique character. Dollis Junior School is both like other primary schools in England, and different from them. But like all communities it will, in time, change again. The following is a snapshot of Dollis as it was in the summer of 2003, at the close of a particularly successful headship which had lasted twenty-five years. Mr D.A. Heasman, headteacher at Dollis since September 1978, was about to retire. What follows is a picture of a thriving, successful, and popular primary school, located on the northern edge of London, in Mill Hill, at the start of the twenty-first century, some fifty years after it first opened.

LEADING THE SCHOOL

OFSTED (Office for Standards in Education) has noted that the leadership of Dollis Junior School is one of its greatest assets, and it has also been identified as one of its particular strengths as a Beacon School. But leadership is much more than just one among other 'assets.' Leadership, focussed in the personality of an individual, is the one factor, more than any other that will make or break any institution. Strong positive leadership has made Dollis Junior School the outstanding success that it is today.

The headteacher himself attributes much of the school's success to an ideal balance between the headteacher, who is left to manage the daily life of the school, and the governors who, while overseeing and regulating the affairs of the school generally, give the headteacher direct support, especially through their committee work. Having been a grant-maintained school, since 1993, Dollis Junior School was re-designated as a foundation school in 1999. Being a foundation school allows Dollis a greater independence than those schools under the direct control of the Barnet Local Education Authority, but this also imposes a greater responsibility for its management on both governors and headteacher. In general terms the governing body, of which the headteacher is himself a member, is responsible for ensuring that Dollis Junior School complies with all Government legislation affecting primary schools. More immediately, it is the governors who employ the school's teachers and support staff, are responsible for the school buildings, all equipment and stores, and a sound budget. On its fiftieth birthday, in 2002, there were sixteen governors, comprising the headteacher, a support staff governor, a teacher governor, two LEA (Local Education Authority) representatives, one co-opted governor, six parent governors and four partnership governors.

The headteacher and the chairman of the governors are in close touch on a daily basis by telephone, and meet informally in the headteacher's office to discuss both general and specific issues. From time to time the headteacher, the chairman and the vice-chairman of the governors meet for a general discussion of school affairs. Steve Harrison, who was chairman for fourteen years (retiring in 2002) was instrumental in guiding the school through to grant-maintained status, and played an important part in the development of the school through the 1990s. The headteacher has described his 'partnership' with Steve Harrison as 'unique'. Steve has been ably followed by Ian Webster, formerly the vice-chairman of the governors.

The governors meet regularly as a whole body three times a year, with additional extraordinary meetings as needed. Much of the work is done by committees, of which there are a few principal ones which meet on a regular basis: finance and general purposes, premises and health and safety, the curriculum committee, and the staffing and appointments committee – this latter assembling when needed as an interview board for new appointments to both teaching and support staff positions, the members being drawn from a pool of available governors. In addition there is a governors' pay committee which meets occasionally, as needed. Other committees, such as those dealing with staff disciplinary matters and school admissions, exist largely on paper, to cover a variety of contingencies – they are rarely, or never, called upon to act. Committee minutes are produced by the headteacher himself, who is present at all meetings, and appear promptly, being normally circulated (except those of the pay committee) to all governors within one week of the meetings. They are sent out on Fridays, with a copy of *School News*.

The headteacher both keeps the governors informed over matters of school business, and also involves them in the school's everyday activities. Governors are encouraged to acquire knowledge of the school curriculum. In addition to the regular meetings of the curriculum committee, and the distribution of its minutes, individual governors have been given a 'link' to one specific area of the curriculum, for example maths, literacy, science and educational visits, SEN (Special Educational Needs) and sex education. There are occasional opportunities to sit in on lessons and to have special demonstrations (of the new interactive electronic whiteboards, for example). At formal governors' meetings there are further opportunities to hear reports from the various teachers acting as curriculum managers, while individual governors have themselves appeared in the classroom as regular guest speakers – notably former chairman (and former Dollis pupil) Steve Harrison, talking on Dollis 'in the old days', and Colin Smith (of Smith's Coffee), bringing his personal knowledge of Kenya to enrich that part of the curriculum studied in year-three classes. There are both many formal invitations to school events, but also, perhaps more importantly numerous informal, and often on the spot invitations to sit in on an assembly, tour the classrooms, meet a new teacher, look in on a special activity, or pop into the headteacher's office for a chat. There is an open invitation to attend INSET days and Beacon training days at the school. Governors are frequent visitors at the school and are active participants in the school's social and fundraising events – on Fun Day they have been the usual source of supply for the chief occupant of Santa's Grotto!

The everyday management of Dollis Junior School is firmly in the hands of its headteacher and deputy headteacher, Derek and Matthew Heasman. As they are also father and son, it must be accounted a special relationship, at once both professional and personal, and one which lies at the heart of Dollis' success.

Derek Heasman began his teaching career in 1954, and in 1968 became the headteacher at Bedmond School, in Hertfordshire. Ten years later he secured the headship of Dollis Junior School. In 2001 a long and successful career as a headteacher was rewarded with an OBE in the Queen's Birthday Honours List. Mr Heasman will be retiring as a headteacher at the end of the 2002/03 academic year, having completed thirty-five years as a headteacher, twenty-five of those years at Dollis Junior School. Mr David Burns, former chief inspector of Barnet's primary schools, will replace him as an acting headteacher from the autumn of 2003.

It is on the shoulders of the headteacher that responsibility falls for the management of the school's material resources, for ensuring that there is a full and properly qualified teaching staff, with adequate support, and that all relevant statutory requirements in respect of primary schools are fully implemented. It is the headteacher who stands ultimately accountable for the quality of the education that the children in his school receive. In the headteacher's own words, his job is a 'multi-faceted' one which he thoroughly enjoys, especially 'all its constant changes'. He sees it as his particular task to be 'a constant encourager and motivator to all', to create and maintain 'a happy and positive school for all pupils and staff.'

The headteacher of Dollis Junior School is responsible for a budget approaching £1,400,000 and Mr Heasman sets as a personal goal, 'to do better than budget'. He has some fifty-two staff to manage, and keeping all staff vacancies (teaching and support) filled, while also taking advantage of opportunities to add additional positions (both temporary and permanent) as appropriate is an ongoing task of the greatest importance. It is essential to establish contacts within the educational community and take initiatives in order to secure good teachers, something Dollis has been remarkably successful at, despite a generally contracting field of candidates in recent years. Whenever possible, prospective teachers are seen personally by the headteacher and/or the deputy headteacher or a senior teacher, in addition to being formally interviewed by a board under the chairmanship of a governor. Applicants for *all* positions (teaching and support, temporary and permanent) at Dollis are formally interviewed.

Despite being funded by the Government, self help has become a virtual necessity for state schools, and fund-raising a fact which headteachers cannot easily avoid. At Dollis, Mr Heasman has taken a leading role in raising funds for the school, and most recently has formed a 'parents' fundraising committee. The weekly *School News* gives prominence on its first page to the current fundraising target, and the latest progress towards it. Over the years, in addition to supplying such items as hall and stage curtains, classroom blinds and playground markings, private funds have enabled Dollis to acquire not only many new library books, computers and related software, but also new minibuses (for school journeys). Fundraising has also made an important contribution to the construction of a computer suite, a new kitchen, a new library and three new classrooms.

Enhancing the general profile of the school in the local community, while establishing a broad network of contacts with potential benefactors, has become another important facet of the headteacher's work at Dollis. The headteacher's efforts to keep Dollis in the public eye are not only important as a basis for raising private funds, but also in 'keeping up pupil numbers', in order to secure the greatest benefit from per capita funding. The school's 'Monday-afternoon visitors', are an educational experience for the children, but also an opportunity to raise the school's profile and to increase the number of the school's 'friends'. Contacts are kept up with local newspapers. Awards, events, activities and special visitors to the school are duly reported on, not least in Dollis' own *School News*, which itself is distributed not only to parents but to a much wider circle of school friends – Her Majesty's Chief Inspector receives a copy, as does the local member of parliament; it is sent as far afield as Singapore.

If the headteacher is busy in his office, he is also deliberate in making time to see people. There is always time for seeing new parents and personally showing them around the school, for dealing with the 'increasing heartaches and problems' of both staff and parents, and for chatting with a child in his office about his or her special interests. This personal contact has done much to establish the special ethos that the school enjoys. When Derek Heasman became the Dollis headteacher in 1978 he interviewed all of the children in the school – a former pupil still recalls that he asked her 'a mathematical question'. All annual reports on the children are read and signed by the headteacher, a task which now involves seeing over 500 of them. By 'tradition' Mr Heasman and his wife Patricia, have met year-three children on their school journey to Ivinghoe, taking them for a climb up the Ivinghoe Beacon. They have also taken smaller groups of children on special visits, most recently (in 2001/02) a year-six 'extension group', whose regular forays took the children behind the scenes at venues as varied as the office of the Chief Commissioner of the Metropolitan Police, the Houses of Parliament, the greenhouses of Finchley Nurseries and the kitchens of the Dorchester Hotel.

To be effective, a leader must have a character which can inspire confidence. Derek Heasman has been an energetic and confident headteacher, intensely proud of *his* school and of his own achievements. Demonstrating the traits of both the showman and the salesman, he has devoted a great deal of time to promoting the school and getting it noticed. Something of his character is apparent in his early 6.30 a.m. start at Dollis each day (governors can expect calls by 7.30 a.m.), having cycled in from his home in Stanmore. His regular production of a weekly *School News*, over a period of many years has been something of a personal mission – on one occasion done from a hospital bed. To say that Derek Heasman is a man of strong religious conviction would be an understatement, for he describes himself as having 'dedicated his life to children and to God'. Although possessing an unpredictable and frequently contradictory character, the headteacher's energy and unwavering belief in being positive is felt throughout the whole school. He is often on the telephone, and while delegating many tasks to others, he keeps a close hand on the work of the school's various regulating committees, producing their minutes himself. He is a headteacher who appears frequently in the corridors and in the classrooms, not least during his daily 'one minute management' tours of inspection.

The deputy headteacher, Matthew Heasman, has been teaching at Dollis since 1989, when he arrived as an NQT. Subsequently he earned an MA in Education, following which he was given the added responsibilities of a senior teacher. Having served twice as an acting deputy headteacher, in 1996 he became deputy headteacher at Dollis, replacing Carol Livingstone who was then both deputy headteacher and SENCO. In 1997 he was in the first thirty candidates to complete the new National Professional Qualification for Headteachers. Most recently he has undertaken training that will qualify him as an OFSTED inspector, and from September 2003 he will take up the post of headteacher at Broadfield Junior School in Hemel Hempstead.

While serving as deputy headteacher at Dollis, Matthew Heasman has been responsible for a wide range of educational and related issues, both new and ongoing. In particular he has been closely involved with all aspects of the curriculum: its planning, the provision of resources, its implementation, and the task of monitoring its progress. His reports are a major part of curriculum committee meetings. Matters concerning the 'quality of teaching and learning' at Dollis have come under his particular scrutiny: to include the direct monitoring of teaching by himself and others, the provision of opportunities for all teaching staff to observe other teachers, especially colleagues, and to receive appropriate further training (an important part of the school's commitment as an Investor in People). He has been responsible for the complex process of setting the annual targets for the year-six SATs, as well as for setting several non-statutory ones as well. The great improvement (since the mid-1990s) in the school's SATs results is owed especially to the efforts of the deputy headteacher. All of this, but especially his attention to the monitoring of 'assessment, recording and reporting' in the school has made him something of a local expert on 'the self-evaluating school', a subject he has lectured on at other schools.

The deputy headteacher has made many of the school's applications for special funds, and has taken on the burden of developing many new school policies. The latter have covered a wide range of educational and social matters, especially in response to Government initiatives, from

'Race Equality' to 'Complaints', from health and safety issues, to the 'Home/School Agreement'. He has been a key figure in taking on the demands of Beacon School status, acting as the co-ordinator for Beacon activities (of which there have been a great number), while also being an active participant in his own right. The deputy headteacher is the key figure in organising the school journeys, and has led many school committees and groups, both regular and ad hoc, from the parents' 'No Bullies Here' focus group to the 'Improve our Playground' committee, to hosting the school's special ethnic curriculum evenings. He also chairs the children's School Council, which meets at least half-termly, and he has been determined to give it an important role in school life. Much of the deputy headteacher's time is given to meeting individual parents. If all of this has not made him busy enough, he has always been ready to step into the breech, to act as a caretaker science manager, to work on the improvement of pupil attendance through better communication with parents and the introduction of attendance awards, to help in training and co-ordinating the mealtime supervisors, or to act as the golden jubilee fête co-ordinator – and even to act as the school crossing patrol. The deputy headteacher regularly covers for absent teachers, doing the equivalent of between half and a full day of teaching every week.

Of special importance to the school has been Matthew Heasman's personal promotion of the Dollis Way code of behaviour (springing from his responsibility for matters of discipline and pupil behaviour) and his belief in promoting good behaviour through positive encouragement. He has acted as friend and counsellor to staff, children, and parents alike, and is generally recognised as a first point of reference for much of what goes on in the school. A combination of energy, dedication, firmness and empathy has made him popular with all members of the Dollis community.

Dollis has been well served by its management structure. The headteacher and the deputy headteacher have a formal agenda meeting once a week, supplemented by many other informal discussions. Management decisions concerning 'strategic policy' are further considered by a 'Leadership Group', comprised of the headteacher, the deputy headteacher, and the two senior teachers, Maurice Markwell and Rita Alak. Additionally the school's 'Senior Management Team', comprising all of the above with the addition of the year leaders, the SENCO, and most recently (since September 2002) the curriculum and assessment co-ordinator, meets on a regular basis as well. And further down the scale the year group teams have weekly meetings for planning, review and evaluation. Working parties and task teams, which may also include governors and interested parents, are also created as need arises. Every Friday, during the lunch break, there is a *short* staff meeting – but always a *full* agenda, informing members of a considerable number of different matters. It is a meeting conducted with energy and pace, and characteristic Dollis humour, to which being a *very full* staff room no doubt contributes!

Ultimately the exercise of authority depends on the personality and character of individuals. Each situation is unique. In the case of Dollis Junior School, the management of many of the daily details, and the strictly academic side of school life, has been undertaken by the deputy headteacher. Importantly, this has enabled the headteacher to devote more attention to matters such as finance, staffing and general resources (all extremely important for a foundation school), while also giving him more time to meet visitors, parents and children. Not least it has enabled him to find the opportunity to produce a weekly *School News*, the value of which is creating a unique school ethos should not be underestimated. The headteacher has been allowed a freedom of action to develop the school's 'profile' in the wider community, and in the widest sense, which in turn has done much to enrich the educational experiences and opportunities for both children and staff. The development, scope, and ultimately the division of responsibilities between the headteacher and his deputy headteacher has been central to making Dollis the successful school that it is, and the headteacher quite rightly describes the contribution of the deputy headteacher as 'colossal'.

The autumn of 2003 will see the departure of both the headteacher and the deputy headteacher, though the former will stay on, part-time, for a further year as a 'director of strategy'. There will then be an acting headteacher, Mr David Burns (former chief inspector of primary schools in Barnet), supported by two acting assistant headteachers, and the director of strategy. Mr Burns, as acting headteacher will be 'operational', with responsibility for 'teaching and learning' while Mr Heasman will be 'strategic', a division of responsibility which will largely replicate the situation that has existed previously between Mr Heasman and his son. The director of strategy will look after financial matters, produce *School News*, arrange and interview the monday afternoon visitor, undertake special projects (which for 2003/04 will involve the construction of three new classrooms), raise funds and handle the school's 'public relations'. The acting headteacher will be concerned specifically with the quality of teaching and the curriculum.

SUPPORTING THE SCHOOL

Dollis has a very strong feeling of family which runs through the whole school, from the headteacher, the deputy headteacher, through the teaching and support staff, to governors, parents and children. All have a part to play. Those who run the school office, serve in the kitchen and are responsible for welfare assistance and for site management play a vital role in school life.

The school office is manned every day from 8.45 a.m. to 5.00 p.m. The school administrator, Kathryn Morrell, is assisted by Androulla Alexander, with further help from Alyson Young. The administrator takes under her wing a wide range of responsibilities from payroll to personnel records, to school registers and the collection of school journey money and permission slips. She deals with the administrative side of job applications and the reception of new staff, prepares letters and reports for the headteacher and others, handles tickets and other administrative matters connected with school productions and other school events, acts as clerk to the governing body, and runs the school shop every Tuesday morning. In 2000 she acted as co-ordinator of that year's Summer Fête. The office staff are also responsible for typing up the weekly *School News*, a task usually undertaken by the administrator's assistant. Kathryn and her assistants are the first point of contact for visitors to the school, and for those phoning in – parents, governors, school suppliers and other outside agencies. There are always queries from children and teachers too. Kathryn quite literally controls entry to the school, as the main entrance 'security door' is operated from the school office. The administrative staff must also be able to use the office computers (there are two of them), a fax machine and the 'reprographic equipment', this later consisting of a Cannon photocopier and a Rioch copy-printer (a speed printer for producing more than twenty copies of a single item), both located nearby in the main stock room. Kathryn started at Dollis Junior School in 1998, and has recently (2003) been awarded a Post Graduate Diploma in Personnel (CIPD) – achieved after two years of part-time study. The administrator's office is at the centre of the daily bustle of school life, a first port of call for parents and visitors, a leading source of information, and a natural meeting place, lying adjacent to both the headteacher's office and the entrance lobby. It is unusual to find the administrator and her assistants alone in the office – the headteacher is one, among many, to be found frequently in its vicinity!

The school's dining hall and kitchen also adjoin the entrance lobby. The Dollis kitchen staff are all employees of Scolarest, a school-meals supplier, part of a larger firm, Compass. The kitchen manager, Victoria Cleary, is a former Dollis Junior pupil who began her culinary career as a general assistant in the Dollis school kitchen in 1990, learning her craft under the direction of the then assistant cook, Joan Murphy, who has been at Dollis since 1985. Subsequently Vicky left

Dollis, but in 1998 returned to take up the post of kitchen manager, with Joan as school cook and assistant manager. Vicky and Joan work in the kitchen full-time, helped by six other part-time assistants. This is a smaller staff than was employed in the 1980s, when the Dollis kitchen was also supplying 300 daily meals to St Vincent's School, and the need to peel and prepare everything fresh gave work to a dozen people. Today potatoes and vegetables come ready peeled.

Over 300 junior children (or about ⅔ of the total at Dollis Junior) eat school meals (of which about ⅓ are free), but the kitchen manager is responsible for the daily production of an average of over 500 dinners, as the kitchen feeds staff and children from both the Dollis Junior and the Dollis Infant schools. This is a considerable undertaking and in the course of ensuring that the meals are ready to serve on time, the manager must see that her staff arrive promptly, that the highest standards of cleanliness are maintained throughout the kitchen, and that the food, being prepared in such large quantities, is cooked at exactly the correct temperature. Once ready, a 'hot cupboard' keeps the food hot. Before serving begins, the manager herself tastes the food. Bookkeeping is also part of the manager's job, she must ensure that all orders received are correct, and make certain that her books balance. The kitchen manager makes up her own menus, which on past occasions have included special promotions, such as food dishes 'from around the world'. Prior to the introduction of the 'Yum Channel' in early 2002, Vicky had to cost each meal she chose; now she can make her selection from a choice of ready-costed meals. If this seems to be quite a lot on Vicky's plate, she has also had to be able to cope with crisis – electrical power failure, and non-delivery by suppliers. Both Vicky and her boss, the senior operations manager of Scolarest, have been interviewed as Monday-afternoon visitors – which certainly led to a greater appreciation of the work of the kitchen manager and her staff. *School News* featured a school kitchen recipe for cakes, and it was decided by the children that the kitchen manager deserved the most poetic of accolades – 'a wonderful star that shines at Dollis'. Dollis school dinners have definitely made progress since the 1950s!

The midday meal, and its associated break time, see much activity as children come and go from the dining hall, and venture outside into the playgrounds. To supervise this busy time of the day, the senior meal time supervisor, Mrs Joyce Campbell, has six meal time supervisors (and a seventh from May 2003). Two of her team do duty in the dining hall itself, a third is stationed at the doors into the school from the lower playground, and the others cover the two playgrounds. As with some of the other support staff, several of the MTS team are also teaching assistants.

Carol Jeffery, the school welfare officer, having started part-time in that post, at Dollis in December 1979, and full-time from February 1980, is the longest serving member of staff apart from the headteacher. She has counselled the distraught, and being fully qualified in first aid, has over the years patched up countless scrapes and bruises, while stopping many a nose bleed along the way. The issuing of health warnings, on such matters as head lice, and the inclusion of timely advice in *School News* on being prepared for hot sunny weather, are all under her watchful eye. Mrs Jeffery's office, the old medical room, used by the school welfare officer since 1979, is just off the museum area, and bears the titles: 'First Aid', 'Medical Room' and 'Lost Property'. It serves as the school's 'lost and found' department, and there is always a small heap of lost sweaters on the small table outside her door; Mrs Jeffery holds regular sales of secondhand Dollis uniforms. Her other regular duties include collecting the dinner money, and the weekly 'printing' of *School News*. Always one for self betterment, she has earned a BA in English, and has most recently completed a two-year Certificate in Counselling Skills, accredited by the National Youth Agency. The headteacher does not hesitate in describing her contribution to the school as 'priceless'.

The everyday maintenance and security of the school buildings are in the very capable hands of the site manager, Dave Hallett. Since starting at Dollis in 1994, Dave has been both the first to arrive at school each day, in order to open up, and the last to leave, being responsible for locking up. Together with Maurice Markwell, who acts as the school's health and safety officer, Dave does a regular site inspection. A wide range of maintenance matters, including the control of the school's new computer-run heating system, fall under Dave's care. He also looks after the school's two minibuses. He deals promptly with day to day repairs, his skills from decorator to carpenter being of great benefit to the school. Nor is this all, for the site manager has also demonstrated his ability at negotiating with contractors and other suppliers, often getting a good bargain for the school. Dave is a key member of the premises committee, attending with voluminous files at the ready, to make his reports and answer questions. Ensuring that the school is always presentable, neat and clean is an important first step in creating a good learning environment, and to this end Dave leads and directs the school's cleaning team – all female, usually four or five, including several who hold other positions too, such as teaching assistant. Dave himself also wears a second hat, and even a third hat, as in addition to being the site manager, he also serves as Dollis's school crossing patrol, and sits on the governing body, as the member for the non-teaching staff. Most recently he has received yet another cap to wear, that of school fire warden. He is always ready to help, can be relied upon to run special errands for the headteacher, and regularly purchases the school's supply of fresh fruit for sale at break times. He also makes regular trips to the school's bank. Prominent in the teachers and governors Fun Day football team, and an active participant in the annual 'Jump Rope for Heart', he well deserves the confidence placed in him, a loyal, hard working and reliable member of staff, and in the headteacher's words, 'wholly dedicated to the school'.

TEACHERS AND CHILDREN

At the start of the twenty-first century Dollis Junior School is the third largest junior school in London (February 2001). The number of children has risen steadily over the last ten years, and today (January 2003) is 513, with a strong waiting list. The number of classes has remained at sixteen (i.e. a four-form entry, producing four classes in each of the school's four year groups, designated years three through six). The rise in pupil numbers has been accommodated by increasing the size of individual classes. Today the average class has thirty-two pupils, with the largest class now having thirty-four.

In addition to the headteacher and the deputy headteacher, there are sixteen full-time class teachers, supported by a fluctuating number of 'support teachers' and 'teaching assistants'. At the time of its fiftieth birthday, in the spring of 2002, the school's 513 children were being taught by sixteen full-time class teachers, with a further nine support teachers working part-time, of whom five had specific responsibilities for children with Special Educational Needs (SEN). In addition the school also employed another fourteen teaching assistants, of whom twelve were part-time and two full-time. In total the headteacher could call upon some twenty-six fully qualified teaching staff (including the deputy headteacher) with a further fourteen teaching assistants (six of whom then had the Certificate for Literacy and Numeracy Support Assistant, or CLANSA). By contrast the entire teaching staff in November 1955 (for 503 children) had consisted of fourteen full-time teachers, for thirteen classes, with the extra teacher being used to make up smaller groups for 'Handwork and Needlework'. The presence of today's support teachers enables the regular class teachers to be released from their class duties for a variety of other tasks and occasions, both within and outside of the school – a newly qualified teacher (NQT) is entitled by law to a regular weekly 'release'. The support teachers are also available to step in when there is an absence due to illness. In 1955, although a temporary supply teacher might be provided by the education authority, the headteacher had on occasion to cover for absent colleagues himself, and in many schools (though not in Dollis) he would have had a regular programme of teaching as well. Today the deputy headteacher, Matthew Heasman, steps in to cover an absence, and regularly does the equivalent of a half to a full day of teaching every week, though neither he nor the headteacher are committed to a regular programme of teaching duties.

The school's children present an ethnic mix which represents most corners of the globe, and this is certainly one of the most obvious contrasts with the school's earlier decades. The local neighbourhoods have changed, and while the ethnic composition of the teaching staff has been less affected, the trend to greater diversity among the pupils has been accelerated in recent years, with a corresponding decline in the proportion of 'white UK heritage' pupils attending the school. In October 2000 there were over thirty different languages other than English being spoken in the homes of Dollis children. When OFSTED visited the school in February 2002, approximately 46 per cent of the pupils were described as coming from ethnic minority groups, and almost 36 per cent of the children came from homes where English was not the first language. Both of these proportions were very much larger than in most schools, and higher than the general proportion (just under 30 per cent) of Barnet residents not born in the United Kingdom. In the spring of 2002 nearly forty different nationalities could be counted, with a growing number of 'refugees and asylum seekers' constituting almost 8 per cent of the school's population. The majority of children were still classified as Christian, but there were 'a very significant number of Hindu and Muslim children', and children of other faiths as well.

Although the school's ethnic composition is now very different from what it was in the past, Dollis Junior School has in fact always had children from a variety of backgrounds, and indeed from countries other than the United Kingdom. The school's admission register for 1964-78 indicates that prior to 1970, about 3 per cent of the children were not native Britons, and of these at least a third were transients, living in the United Kingdom only temporarily, usually on account of their father's employment. Through the 1970s the number of non-British names appearing in the school register increased, coming to represent about 10 per cent of all those enrolled over the years of Mr L.H. Patterson's headship, 1964-1978. Many were at Dollis only a short time, among them were children from the United States of America, Australia and Japan. Other nationalities appeared, too: from continental Europe there were occasional children from France, Belgium, Spain and Italy; others were from South America, from Brazil, Chile and Venezuela. Israel, Kuwait and Afghanistan were also represented, as was South Africa and Malaya. Indian names began appearing, among them were children from families expelled from Uganda in 1972. Today the social background of the children is more diverse than ever. Although there are some children from very privileged backgrounds, more than one in five of the children are in circumstances which entitle them to free school meals. This is a proportion which is similar, if slightly higher, than the national average.

For many years children from army families living at Inglis Barracks formed a distinct element in the school's population. They made up a sizable part of the pupil numbers. From the end of 1965, and through the following two years, large numbers of army children were enrolled at Dollis. The school register of 1964-78 shows children from these army families making up nearly 30 per cent of the Dollis children. At the beginning of that period more than one in three of Dollis Junior children were from service families, this proportion dropping in the last years to one in five. The children came and went as their fathers were posted abroad or were returned to Britain. Many arrived from Germany, others from Gibraltar, Malta and Cyprus, and from much further afield too, from Aden, Hong Kong and Singapore. The turnover was always high – over the course of the 1973/74 year alone, there were fifty-one casual admissions and forty-one departures. Today (2003) the army barely maintains a presence in the barracks area, and only a handful of children from service families attend Dollis.

GETTING TO SCHOOL

Dollis has always been a local school, drawing the majority of its children from the immediate neighbourhood. From 1964 to 1969, some 57 per cent of the children lived within half a mile of the school, and almost all of those who attended were within one mile. Slightly over 1 per cent lived beyond this, the most distant children being about two miles away, at Woodside and on Hendon Wood Lane. Fifty per cent of the children came from the Brookfield estate, the Bittacy and Devonshire Road areas. The Inglis Barracks, as already mentioned, accounted for over 33 per cent. The situation was little changed in the following years. From 1976 through 1978, the figures were quite similar: 60 per cent lived within half a mile, about 95 per cent within one mile. Some 53 per cent came from the Brookfield estate, the Bittacy area and the Devonshire Road area, and a further 20 per cent from the Inglis Barracks. There was, however, in these statistics a change which was pointing to the future. Almost 5 per cent were now living more than one mile from the school and the furthest of these outliers was now 3½ miles away in the Canons Park area, while another was in Little Stanmore, and a third came from North Finchley. Almost imperceptibly, the catchment area was spreading. In October 2001, Dollis was still drawing the greatest number of its pupils from those areas closest to the school, as it has always done, but a much larger proportion were coming from further away, from Edgware, Burnt Oak and Colindale, and others from further still, from Cricklewood, Muswell Hill, Bush Hill Park and Barnet.

In the past the great majority of primary age children travelled to and from school on their own. In 1970 some 80 per cent of children did so, but in more recent years this has been completely reversed. By 1990 approximately 91 per cent came with an adult, leaving only 9 per cent who still travelled on their own. And whereas in the past children had usually walked to school, now an ever increasing number are driven to school by mum or dad, in what has been labelled 'the school run'. Surveys suggest that the school run has increased rush hour traffic in Britain by as much as 20 per cent – a result of the ever-growing ownership of cars (including the phenomenon of the two car family), linked to heightened concern over the safety of children, on account of the increased volume of traffic (!), and worry over the real or imagined threat of 'strangers' bent on harming young children. Moreover, the growing ownership of cars has enabled more children to live further away from those schools whose catchment areas are not tightly prescribed. At Dollis Junior School there are now more children living further away than ever before, making a trip by car seem more of an imperative than a choice, when faced with a journey of perhaps 8 miles or more. In 1999 the Borough of Barnet started promoting a Walk to School Week in an attempt to get more parents and minders to leave their vehicles at home, if only for five days of the year. Dollis has been an active participant, with children and parents being provided with 'diaries', supplied by the Borough of Barnet, to record a week's observations on the advantages of walking.

THE NATIONAL CURRICULUM AND BEYOND

Dollis follows the programme for Key Stage Two as laid out in the Government's National Curriculum for children aged seven to eleven. The subjects taught are divided between those considered to be 'core subjects' (English, mathematics and science) and those designated as 'non-core foundation subjects' (design and technology, information and communication technology or ICT, history, geography, art and design, music and physical education). In addition there is some religious instruction (which involves looking at four different faiths – Hinduism, Islam,

Judaism and Christianity), and a miscellany covered under PSHE (personal, social and health education). At Dollis each area of the curriculum has a teacher, selected by interview, who acts as that subject's 'manager'. Such appointments entail planning and budgetary responsibilities. There is a governor's curriculum committee which meets regularly to keep abreast of changes, and to hear reports from the school's curriculum managers.

As core subjects, English, mathematics and science receive the greatest attention. English has a 'literacy hour' on four days of the week, with 'extended writing' lessons on the fifth, while mathematics gets its daily 'numeracy lesson'. To further promote reading, three 'book fairs' are held in the school hall during the year, to coincide with the parents' open evenings at the school. By comparison, history, geography, music and art and design receive far less attention in the regular lesson schedule. This is something many teachers regret, and Dollis makes considerable effort whenever possible to give more emphasis to these subjects. Various lessons are 'tied in' with each other, for example year five's history lessons on Victorian Britain have been tied in with art lessons on William Morris, design and technology sessions on creating a model of a Victorian house, and with a musical appreciation of the repertoire of the Victorian music hall. Notably there are a number of special activities and events, some occurring on a regular basis, others as unique occasions, which promote 'non-core' subjects. Indeed all aspects of the curriculum benefit greatly from the variety and number of such events, as well as from school day trips, school clubs and residential journeys.

Clubs, both after school and during the lunch break, are another means of enhancing the curriculum. Apart from English, no modern languages are taught at Dollis, but through a lunchtime club run by La Petite Ecole, some children can at least get a first taste of speaking and listening to French. Another lunchtime club, the Laser Beams, is a Christian club which offers a further chance to explore the Bible. There is a first aid club, whose members have entered regional competitions with great success, and also a chess club. Physical education is given an extra boost through a variety of clubs and sports teams: two judo clubs, several football teams (including a girls' team), a netball team, a gymnastics team and a tag rugby club. Inter-school sports competitions are well reported in *School News*, and in the summer term a great deal of enthusiasm is generated by the school's annual sports day and swimming galas (held at the Copthall pool).

There are special weeks set aside, usually one in the autumn, when the whole of that week's lessons and activities are centred on one area of the curriculum. Such occasions have been very well received by both parents and children – art, history and science have all benefited in recent years. There is also a regular programme of 'living history days', which, through the enthusiasm of Alison Sharpe, the history manager, has done much to raise the profile of history in the school. The teachers and children of a particular year group come to school in appropriate costume, and spend the day on lessons and activities which have been carefully tied into the historical period they are then studying. Such days offer opportunities for artistic creation and craft work too, and are always occasions of great excitement and enjoyment. History and geography are again given special emphasis on many class visits (to the British Museum for example), and especially on the residential journeys, which always include some appreciation of local geography, and time at historic sites.

Through the efforts of the school's music manager, Colin Dowland, music is given a very high profile in school life, despite it being allowed little formal lesson time. Lunchtimes are used to sustain both a senior and a junior choir, a wind band and a string group. In June 2002 the borough's peripatetic music teachers were giving instrumental instruction to 147 Dollis children – over 28 per cent of all the children in the school. To the great enjoyment of both children and parents, the school maintains a full musical calendar which tries each year to include both a lower-school and an upper-school production, the latter often reaching a remarkably high standard. Music, singing, drama and dance are skilfully combined, not a few of the scripts and choreography being written and devised entirely within Dollis, in great measure owing to the talent and enthusiasm of Mr Dowland. In addition there is a 'Cabaret Night' in the spring term, and a 'Summer Serenade' concert (two nights), both of which feature individual performers. Any mention of music at Dollis would not, however, be complete without special reference to the 'Dollis Deepans' steel-pans band. While the violin is the most popular instrument being learned at Dollis, second on the list are the steel pans. The Dollis Deepans, now almost ten years old, have in many ways become a hallmark of the school, their performances always finishing amidst a rapturous applause which is well deserved. Over the years the Deepans have had many musical successes, including a trip to Slovenia, a recording for BBC Radio, and appearances at the Royal Festival Hall and at Lords' Cricket Ground. The Deepans have also taken part in the finals of the National Youth Festival. The emergence of a steel pan group at neighbouring Copthall secondary school owes its inception to former Dollis pupils.

The school's programme of residential school journeys is noteworthy, as Dollis runs a full slate of such ventures, allowing each of the school's sixteen classes to make one such journey every year (during the spring and summer terms). Thanks to the initiative and enthusiasm of the headteacher, Dollis children have been enjoying such residential excursions for over twenty years. In the early 1980s the undertaking of such trips was down to individual teachers, the itineraries being drawn up to suit their particular classes. Today, trip itineraries are planned for a whole year group, the process being very much a team effort. As every class in the school takes to the road in turn, the whole programme must be carefully arranged and co-ordinated, a task which has been ably undertaken by the deputy headteacher. Each journey is planned and prepared months in advance. Money and consent forms must be collected, and meetings held to inform parents of particular details. Arranging the staffing cover is itself a considerable chore, as each class is accompanied by two class teachers, plus other adult helpers. Every year group takes part, with the journeys becoming progressively more ambitious as the children get older. Year-three classes travel to Ivinghoe in Buckinghamshire and spend one night there – for many children it is often the first time away from home on their own. Year-four classes venture into Essex to Castle Hedingham, spending two nights away, while year five treks into Derbyshire for three nights and four days, and year-six ventures into Wales, to the Brecon Beacons, for a full week: four nights and five days away. Each journey encompasses a wide variety of educational visits and activities, from nature and ecology studies, to mines and museums, castles, churches and canals. The children work hard during these visits, but there are moments just for fun, too. Before each trip, lesson time is spent preparing the children for what they will see and do, and once they have returned, more hours will be spent in school and at home writing up and illustrating (often voluminous!) journey reports. This very ambitious programme of residential journeys is only possible through the time and effort put in by the teachers (who every year reconnoitre each journey), and because there are parents willing to help, not least with driving the school's two minibuses. Each journey is fully described in *School News*, often by an accompanying parent, and messages received from classes while 'on school journey' are duly reported to the whole school in assembly. Dollis' residential school journey programme is something the school is justifiably proud of.

The school's regular 'Monday-afternoon visitor' is a further feature of Dollis school life which must be singled out for particular mention. It not only broadens the children's general knowledge of the world beyond the school environment, but also encourages children through example, to set high goals for themselves. Often too, it directly enhances certain aspects of the school curriculum. Begun by the headteacher in 1987, the Monday-afternoon visitor is an invited guest who comes to the school at the invitation of the headteacher, in order to be introduced, and then 'interviewed' by the children in a special assembly. The visits are always an occasion of interest and anticipation, as many of the 'visitors' are well-known national, and even international, personalities. But the visitors include people from all walks of life: the London taxi driver and the soldier are represented alongside medical practioneers, judges, members of the Queen's household, officers of parliament, prominent sportsmen, business executives, TV and film personalities. All of the interviews are written up by the week's 'reporters', chosen from the year-six children, with selected extracts appearing every Friday in the headteacher's *School News*.

CLASSROOMS, COMPUTERS AND SPECIAL NEEDS

Dollis today has sixteen regular classrooms (the nine original rooms, with three more added in 1994, plus another four classrooms in the 'huts', the two mobile classrooms of 1967 and 1968, and a double hut received from Ravenscroft School in 1993). There are also two dedicated SEN (Special Educational Needs) rooms, created in the main cross-corridor from former cloakroom space – prior to their creation children with 'special needs' were given tuition in the 'steelpans' hut' on the lower playground.

The dual-locker desks of the past have given way to small tables, which can accommodate several children at each, and may be arranged according to the class teacher's choice. Commonly the tables (say about sixteen in total) are put together to create various sized groups of children, the groups of tables so formed being spaced across the room, not necessarily with regard to a formal pattern. The older notion of orderly rows still finds occasional favour, as do more unusual arrangements such as that of setting the tables out in a large horseshoe stretching around the room. There will be a desk for the teacher, and various book shelves around the room – for the teacher's own books, for children's work books, and for children's reading and reference books (the 'book corner'). Each child is assigned a plastic tray in which work sheets and certain work books are to be kept, the trays being either stored in specially made sets of shelves, or each tray sliding separately under the table tops.

Display is an important feature of every classroom, as indeed it is throughout the school (hall and corridors). One of Mr Heasman's first acts as the new headteacher at Dollis in 1978 was to have display boards placed in the public areas of the school. Today there are displays of children's art, writing and craft projects, of specific topics being studied, and of recent trips. In the main entrance lobby there are further displays of children's work, including a special space between the doors leading into the hall for the display of work considered to be outstanding. Within the classrooms, in addition to using walls and shelves, one popular method of display is by the suspension of a cord, stretched overhead across the room, on which might be fixed 'a history time line', or other subject information, or a further selection of the children's own work. Classrooms are kept extremely neat and tidy, and certain areas might be labelled, for example a corner for 'art and design'. Each room has its own small storeroom.

Dollis classrooms are equipped with both the traditional blackboard, and a more recent version, the whiteboard. Each classroom has an internet linked window box computer and printer, replacing the school's older Dell models, which are now to be found plugged in along the finger corridors, loaded with the self running RM maths system. Much importance has been placed on the introduction of ICT into primary schools, and in addition to those computers in the classrooms and corridors, Dollis also has an ICT suite, opened in 2000. All classes have a weekly ICT lesson on the suite's seventeen window box computers, all internet linked, with printers, two scanners and a data projector. The suite is also available for further class use on other curriculum subjects as well. Elsewhere, the school office has two computers, with full internet access, the library has two as well, while the SEN rooms, music room, headteacher and deputy headteacher are also online with their own computers. Laptop computers have also made an appearance in the school: eleven are in use by SEN children who have difficulty in forming hand written letters, and another four have been given out to new teachers. The school has its own web site, and all staff members have their own e-mail addresses.

Great emphasis has been put on developing the use of computers in all areas of the curriculum. 'Computer literacy' has become a further skill which every primary school teacher must have, and acquiring at least one teacher who has special computer knowledge and expertise has become essential for every school. The last few years have seen a great expansion in the use of computers at Dollis, and the school has been very fortunate in its resident computer expert, Elaine Geeves. She has been responsible for the selection, installation and maintenance of the school's current computer hardware, the acquisition of appropriate software, and for ensuring that ICT skills are being taught to all members of the teaching staff.

The full impact of the internet linked computer on society generally, and on learning in the classroom in particular, has yet to be seen and fully understood. The Government's target for the provision of computers in primary schools is set at one computer for seven pupils by the summer of 2005. To achieve such a goal will require a great deal of new expenditure (while also maintaining and replacing the existing stock of computers at the same time). The current ratio of internet linked computers available in the classrooms and the ICT suite at Dollis, stands at one computer for every fifteen pupils. The introduction of computer technology into schools has been expensive, and only now is the full impact of the ongoing costs of maintenance and replacement being realised. Yet even as this is occurring, the primary school classroom is poised on the edge of what would seem to be yet another, expensive, technological 'revolution', the 'interactive electronic whiteboard', which quite literally transfers greatly magnified images directly from the computer screen to the front of the classroom, while also making them 'interactive' – responsive to the touch of teacher and pupil. 'Chalk and talk' seems set to become 'touch and tell'. The children are captivated, but the cost, currently at £5,000 per board, with its projector, is not inconsiderable. At the moment they are a rarity, but Dollis has been extremely fortunate in being able to install five such interactive whiteboards in the course of 2002, and a further two in 2003. A portion of the funds derived from Dollis's status as a Beacon school, have been used for this project, and the results put on show for teachers from other schools to see. Elaine Geeves has led the introduction and demonstration of the new electronic whiteboards.

Much attention is currently focussed on computers and their potential as an educational tool, but Dollis has not neglected other resources which, if not so much in the limelight, are important school assets. A great deal of effort is put into encouraging children to read and to value books, and an integral part of this promotion has been the recent improvement of the school library, presently located in what was formerly the year-six boys' cloakroom. In November 1999 a refurbished, and computer equipped, 'new' library was officially opened. The following autumn, thanks to a grant from the New Opportunities Fund, to create a lunchtime 'Open Library Club' and an after-school 'Homework Club', the school was able for the first time to add a part-time librarian to the staff. This special funding came to an end after two years, but the school has continued both the clubs and the librarian, meeting the costs from the school's own budget. The acquisition of a librarian has been an important step in raising the profile of the library, but new technology for the library has also given it a distinct boost. While many Barnet primary schools are still using a manual system of tickets for borrowing and returning books, Dollis has moved in the short space of a few years, since 1999, from tickets, to a computer based system using the electronic scanning of bar codes, and most recently to a high specification computer and the very latest technology, the Micro Librarian Fingerprint System, which enables each individual's transactions to be recorded by simply touching a special sensor. Introduced in 2002, Dollis is ostensibly the first Barnet primary school operating such a system. Currently the library has over 6,500 books plus a collection of songs and stories on tape.

In addition to the library, special mention must also be made of the school's museum, whose peripatetic existence (from 'hut' to storage room), was finally ended in January 1999 when a dedicated space just outside of the welfare office, recessed from the corridor, was officially opened by the area manager of HSBC, the museum's sponsor. The museum has a growing collection of both everyday domestic objects, and of items specifically of Dollis school interest. Displays are used to encourage a general interest in history, and to support specific parts of the curriculum. Looking through the windows opposite the museum area, one of the school's other resources can be seen: The Lea Caetano nature garden and pond, opened in 2000 in memory of a year-six child who died very suddenly at the start of the previous autumn term. Since 1983 the school has also had a 'nature reserve' just outside of the school grounds, on a part of the old disused railway line. Nearby Copthall Pool offers excellent facilities for swimming lessons.

The class teacher of today enjoys a level of support in the classroom undreamt of in decades past. In the 1950s a school would be fortunate if it could muster a 'floating teacher' who could help out when a colleague went absent, or a smaller class was needed for a particular lesson. Today's class teacher can draw on a number of different helpmates: SEN specialists, general support teachers and teaching assistants. In the spring of 2002 Dollis Junior School had a formidable array of such classroom support: one SEN teacher and co-ordinator (SENCO), one SEN teacher, six general support teachers, two learning support teachers and fourteen teaching assistants. Several of these positions are full-time, but most are on a part-time basis, varying from as little as a few hours a week to virtually a full five-day week; most are for several days each week. The number of such support staff fluctuates with the availability of funds, but the overall trend of recent years has been one of steadily increasing numbers. There were six classroom assistants in 1995, in the autumn of 1999 there were seven, and in the spring of 2001 there were eleven. As with the regular class teachers generally, most of the support teaching staff are female – of the fourteen teaching assistants of 2002, only two were men.

Whereas in the past, children with behavioural problems and learning difficulties received little attention – occasionally a child with a very obvious problem might be sent to one of a few special schools – today their needs are closely monitored and must be attended to, in accordance with the Disability Discrimination Act 1995 and the SEN and Disability Act 2001. This is both a benefit to the class teacher and to the child. All Dollis children are carefully scrutinised, and where appropriate included on an SEN register, its entries running from a 'record of concern', through learning difficulties which can be addressed within the school, to special medical conditions and situations which can require help from outside agencies. In the summer term of 2002 a total of 151 children were on the register: seventeen required some sort of outside assistance, and four had special 'statemented' conditions. Individual children and small groups can be taught separately in the school's two SEN rooms, while in the classrooms themselves there is direct help from support teachers and teaching assistants. Working closely with classroom teachers, the teaching assistants at Dollis help less able children to understand, and encourage them to participate in a lesson as it progresses. They help the inattentive child to concentrate, they answer children's questions during independent work time, and listen to children reading. It is a task which requires tact, patience and adaptability, and the school encourages its teaching assistants to undertake training themselves – six of them now have a CLANSA qualification, i.e. the Certificate for Literacy and Numeracy Support Assistants. They also help teachers prepare lesson materials by undertaking such tasks as the photocopying of work sheets. The Dollis SENCO, Janice Rolnick, has set a high standard for her own work, and the same effort and dedication is seen in the teaching assistants, whose work she is responsible for monitoring. SEN is well supported, but it remains an open question as to how best to support the children at the other end of the spectrum, the most able and gifted children.

LEARNING FOR ALL

In accord with its Investor in People award (recently given for the third time) Dollis actively encourages *all* of its staff to seek further qualifications and to develop their personal careers. At interview, candidates for all school positions are encouraged to talk about their future plans and asked specifically if they would be interested in pursuing further qualifications. This is taken up again by the headteacher, who holds professional development interviews with all staff members.

The size and organisation of the school allows valuable opportunities for teachers to experience responsibility beyond their own classrooms, by becoming a subject manager, or to gain leadership experience by acting as a year leader and assuming responsibility for the planning and implementation of a curriculum for all four classes of a year group. On more formal lines, the school maintains a regular programme of 'professional development' for its teachers. As in all schools there is a regular series of training sessions within the school itself. During the autumn and spring terms there are five INSET (In Service Training) days, and a further number of much shorter 'twilight sessions' held after school hours. Such sessions might be run by a Dollis staff member, or by an outside speaker, and cover a wide variety of topics related to primary school teaching, from the implementation of specific Government initiatives, to classroom management and ICT skills. One of the INSET days is always devoted to working on the annual School Improvement Plan. In addition all staff, teaching and other staff are actively encouraged to take outside courses relevant to their interests and aspirations. Class teachers and support teachers attend a wide range of courses, as do the school's teaching assistants. The meal-time supervisors, the office staff, the site manager and the school's welfare officer have all attended special courses to either enhance their skills and knowledge, or specifically to acquire particular qualifications. These have been both single-day courses and much longer quests for certificates and diplomas. The desire to better oneself seems to be an infectious condition – and the personal achievement of many individuals has been noteworthy.

The school's acquisition of Beacon status in 2001 has added yet another dimension to Dollis as a place of learning – for teachers themselves, and for others. Beacon funds have enabled the school to hold several special day courses, given by outside speakers, which have attracted a very full audience of teachers, from both Dollis Junior School itself, Dollis Infant School, and from many other Barnet schools as well. Beacon status has meant that Dollis teachers go to other schools to offer advice, and to give courses. Rita Alak shares her expertise as an advanced skills teacher – her attainment of this qualification in 1999 made her the first AST in Barnet and one of the first thirty nationally. The deputy headteacher has talked on 'The Self Evaluating School', and the Dollis SENCO, Janice Rolnick, has spoken and run courses on various aspects of her SEN work. Indeed Mrs Rolnick has been prominent in the school's Beacon activities. Dollis has always welcomed visits from other teachers and educationalists, and Beacon status has enriched this side of Dollis life still further, enabling class teachers to act as host and exemplar to colleagues from other schools. The list of visitors is an extensive one, and has recently included NPQH (National Professional Qualification for Headteachers) trainees, PGCE (Post Graduate Certificate in Education) students on observation weeks and on practice training, and prospective candidates for the Government's 'Open Schools Programme', intended to recruit new teachers. There have been students studying various aspects of child behaviour, and on one occasion twenty-two teachers from the Priory School, Slough, spent one of their INSET days at Dollis, to see the teaching, and to learn about the school's organisation and management systems. Foreign visitors too frequently find their way to Dollis – groups of Dutch and German student teachers, a succession of American teachers (especially from the Graff family!), teachers from Japan, and the ministers of education of both Singapore and Qatar.

DISCIPLINE: AN EMPHASIS ON THE POSITIVE

Matters of discipline and punishment loom large in many memories of school life, not least in former Dollis pupils who knew the school in past decades. Corporal punishment in schools was a recurring topic of debate for many years, but not until 1986 did parliament finally vote in favour of its abolition. The use of the slipper, the ruler, and a cuff round the ears may be a thing of the past, but the need to maintain order and to promote good behaviour in the classroom remains essential if children are to have a calm environment in which they can learn.

To attain that order and good behaviour Dollis places 'an emphasis on the positive'. The school's policy on 'Behaviour and Discipline' has at its core a desire to 'catch children being good'. To this end teachers are encouraged to express high expectations for all pupils, in academic achievement and in general behaviour. Children are expected to take a measure of responsibility for their own behaviour, to set goals for themselves, reflect on their progress, and to respect and to work co-operatively with others. Learning good behaviour and becoming a responsible member of society, is taken to be as much a part of a child's education as learning to read and write, and the classroom is seen as a practical setting in which a child can acquire good social skills.

Clearly understood procedures, both within the classroom and in the school as a whole, are essential for creating a climate in which good behaviour can be established and maintained. At Dollis the tone for the day is set each morning when the children, who have gathered in the playground before the start of school, hear the ringing of the school bell by the teacher on duty. Through requiring each child to stand still immediately, and to remain motionless where they are, separate from others, while listening for the signal for their year group to proceed into the school, each child is reminded in a most effective manner, both that school has now commenced, and that they alone are now responsible for their own conduct. Though perhaps seeming to be a small detail, it is through the accumulation of many such purposeful details, that good order and discipline are established.

There are specific rules governing such things as movement and general conduct in the school corridors, and there are other rules specific to the dining hall, and to assemblies in the school hall (which with over 500 children, are miracles of compression!). The rules and procedures laid down by each class teacher are often supplemented by a set of special 'class rules', devised by the children themselves, for use within their particular room. Similarly a set of Playground Rules has been drawn up by the children who make up the School Council, and these are displayed prominently in the playground. They are a mix of specific rules and a general code of behaviour.

Underpinning all of the school's specific rules and procedures, is a general code of personal behaviour: The Dollis Way. Indeed it is not too much to say that the tenets of the Dollis Way have become a central feature of school life. Starting out in 1997 as the 'Golden Rules', the code was refashioned and re-christened as The Dollis Way two years later. The Dollis Way was introduced to the school by the deputy headteacher in an assembly in October 1999, and receives regular attention through discussion in whole school assemblies and year group meetings, through its frequent mention and appearance in the weekly *School News*, and through being displayed throughout the school. Copies are also sent home with the children – and cases are known of them being prominently displayed for the guidance of the whole family! The code, linked by name to the school itself, has been highly successful in promoting good behaviour, and in further fostering a school spirit, for there can be a 'Dollis Way' of doing everything.

In keeping with the school's 'emphasis on the positive', rewards for effort, for good behaviour and for achievement form an integral part of Dollis life. All members of staff, both teaching and support, are encouraged to reward good behaviour. Frequently this is verbal praise, but a variety of more formal reward schemes are also used. In class there are stars, ticks, points, smiley faces or certificates to be earned according to criteria set by the teachers. Achievement is also rewarded by 'golden time' (being allowed to choose an activity) or by being given special responsibility, such as looking after a class pet, or running a special errand. At the end of each term, whole-class awards are given for the highest percentage attendance and for the lowest percentage of lates: the winning class receives a framed certificate. Individuals with 100 per cent attendance are awarded separate certificates, given out by the headteacher in assembly. Various incentives are used to reward good playground behaviour, while meal time supervisors have their own 'Friday lunchtime certificates' and stickers for individual children. Year group leaders have their own reward systems, and the year groups hold regular 'praise meetings' in which individuals are awarded badges or certificates. Special certificates – gold, silver and bronze – are awarded for behaviour on the residential school journeys. The school assembly is another regular occasion used for bestowing public praise, as are the pages of the weekly *School News*, which note the achievements of children both within the school and without, in the wider community. *School News* reproduces exceptional written work and regularly reports on the interests and activities of individual children in the headteacher's 'Time for a Chat'. There are often children at the headteacher's door, waiting for 'a time to chat'!

Much effort is put into recognising and rewarding good behaviour but as surely as good behaviour is to be praised, it must always be made clear that bad behaviour is unacceptable and will be punished. Most problems can be dealt with on the spot. Usually a few words from the class teacher or other staff member are sufficient, but further action can include separating a child from others in the classroom, excluding them from some or all activities for a fixed period of time. Extra homework might be given, or a child made to miss all or part of a playtime. A child can also be sent to work in another class for a short 'cooling off' period (a green card), or for an entire lesson (a red card). For offences committed during playtime, a child can be asked to stand against 'the wall' (the wall being in the cross corridor which is opposite the main playground doors), for a specific time, before going out again to play. Should such minor punishments, and being 'told off', fail to produce an improvement, the next step is to send the offender to the year leader, or perhaps to another teacher in the same year group.

For particularly aggressive or offensive behaviour (such as pushing, kicking or swearing), or for persistent disobedience, a pupil is sent to Friday Club. Details are entered into the Friday Club Book, and the culprit is seen by the deputy headteacher or a senior teacher, on a Friday morning. Should a child's name appear in the Friday Club Book three times in one term, a letter is sent to the parents or guardians. If the offender's name appears six times in a term, then the parents (or guardians) are invited to school for a formal interview with the deputy headteacher. At the end of each term the Friday Club record is wiped clean. Should still further action be required, parents might be requested to be ready to supervise, or even to remove their child from the school premises. Exclusion – lunchtime exclusions, temporary and ultimately permanent exclusions – would in exceptional cases constitute the final stage. Such action has been extremely rare and unusual at Dollis.

The good behaviour of Dollis Junior School children is often remarked upon by both visitors to the school, and by those who see them on school visits and journeys. Much is certainly due to the consistent effort made across the whole school to manage the behaviour of the children. It is made clear to both staff and children at Dollis that *all* of members of the school staff, whether teaching or support, are involved in managing the behaviour of *all* the school's children. To this end class teachers do not confine verbal correction or praise to 'their' children alone – a very desirable situation much encouraged by the year-group system. But Dollis also makes every effort to involve those other key players – the parents and guardians – in the management of behaviour. The school goes to great lengths to make every aspect of its teaching and management accessible to parents, and to express a clear desire that parents, pupils and staff work together to ensure good standards of pupil behaviour. In this regard the Government's introduction in 1999 of a 'Home/School Agreement' was embraced as another opportunity to make and strengthen the bonds between the school and each child's home. The Dollis version, produced by a working party of parents and teachers under the deputy headteacher, sets out the responsibilities of pupil, parent and school with care and clarity.

Dollis children are proud of their school. Attention is paid to the correct wearing of school uniform, which both encourages a collective spirit, and an individual pride, especially if the headteacher compliments you on a smart appearance! Pride in being a pupil at a particular school and being a member of a particular teacher's class, can help greatly in creating and sustaining good behaviour. At Dollis, children are frequently told to be 'good ambassadors' for their school, especially when going out on trips, and the results would suggest that many children do take such an injunction to heart.

THE SCHOOL YEAR

The first of the year's three terms commences in early September. The day preceding the arrival of the children is given over to a gathering of teachers and other staff for the first INSET day of the new academic year. The occasion serves as an opportunity for the headteacher to welcome new staff members, to go over an outline of the year ahead, to discuss plans, and to encourage all staff at the start of another year. It is the first of a number of INSET days held through the year each devoted to a different theme concerned with some aspect of primary school teaching. The following day, the relative tranquillity of this first INSET gathering is replaced by the excitement of the children as they congregate in the school playground, ready for their first day of the autumn term.

In the early weeks, teachers and children get to know each other, and in the first two weeks of October the school holds a parent/teacher consultation, a chance for parents to meet their child's new class teacher. This is an 'open evening', with a schedule of prearranged timed meetings, each intended to be but 'five minutes' – invariably an optimistic target! These consultations are the first of three, one being held in each of the school terms – in between times teachers are available to see parents by appointment. While the parents queue in the corridors, waiting their turn, a book sale (provided from outside of the school) is held in the school hall.

Dollis is a busy, active school, with a full and eventful roster of occasions, both regular happenings and special events. One of the regular autumn visitors to Dollis is the school photographer, who makes an appearance about the end of September in order to take individual portraits of children and staff. Another visit is made later in the year, in the spring, to take class, team and club photographs. Late September is also the time for the first of the school's regular charity events. Towards the end of the month the school participates in the annual Macmillan Nurses' Coffee Morning. The school's special autumn 'harvest assembly' is used to collect gifts of food for dispatch to Eastern European countries, and in the summer term, in June, the school supports the 'Jump Rope for Heart', an event which gets the whole school, always including the headteacher, skipping rope to raise money for the British Heart Foundation. In 2003 the school raised £3,301.48. In October a chosen group of forty Dollis children, taken from across the year groups, make a day long visit to the Japanese School in Acton, a visit which is reciprocated in June by a similar group of Japanese children coming to Dollis. This has been a regular annual exchange since the early 1990s. The visits start with a presentation by the guests, after which each of the guests is paired off with a host child for the rest of the day.

During the autumn and the spring terms the whole school assembles in the hall each week to meet the week's 'Monday-afternoon visitor' – a special guest who comes to the school at the invitation of the headteacher, in order to be introduced and then 'interviewed' by the children. These special visits start in September and are always occasions of much interest, not least to the parents who can read the results later in *School News*!

For the children one of the highlights of the autumn term must be Fun Day, held on a Saturday in the latter part of November. Anticipation builds through the term, especially in the preceding weeks when the call goes out for unwanted books, games and toys! As the day itself approaches the number of bulging plastic bags set down each morning in the entrance lobby increases, with prizes for the class which brings in the most 'bags of bits'. Elsewhere, in the 'Steel Pans' Hut', on the edge of the lower playground, the mountain of such bags grows and groans, with one or two parent volunteers attempting to sort it out – if indeed they can get in at all! Fun Day begins about 10.30 a.m. with football and netball matches involving teachers, parents and governors. Lunches are on sale, and the afternoon is given over to a Christmas Bazaar, complete with 'Santa's Grotto', raffles, tombola, games of chance, cake, plant, bric-a-brac and book stalls, and toys by the heap, all at 'irresistible' prices, though there always seem to be great number left over too! The day is well supported by staff, parents and governors, many of whom are manning the stalls and various activities. The school is thronged with parents and children, the latter pleased to be returning home with bulging bags of goodies – many being the same plastic bags in which those very goodies first arrived at school! The day closes about 3.30 to 4.00 p.m., with the presentation of raffle prizes, followed by the inevitable clear up – accomplished in fairly short order through some good-humoured team work with sweeper, handcart and hoover.

In December, the final month of the autumn term, thoughts turn to Christmas. The headteacher sets a Christmas acrostic challenge in the *School News*, Christmas poems begin to appear, and a Christmas post box, a Dollis tradition since the first one appeared in December 1980, is set up in the entrance lobby to receive cards for delivery within the school by the year-six children. A special Christmas lunch is prepared by the school kitchen staff, and the season is further celebrated by class parties. A Christmas assembly is held towards the end of term. This festive month is also the occasion for the first of the year's music and drama productions, in this case by the lower school, i.e. those children in years three and four.

Following the Christmas break, the spring term begins in early January. As in the autumn term, there is another INSET day, followed the next day by the commencement of actual classes. The spring term is marked by a number of regular events. The year-five children learn something of the pride, pitfalls and responsibilities of parenthood, when they spend a day 'nursing' their own little charge – an egg (!) – on the appropriately named 'Egg Day'. Each egg is given a name and its own biographical details. In mid-February the children's own parents meet up with the teachers for a second teacher/parent consultation. The year's progress thus far is reviewed, and 'targets' are set for the remaining half year. On a lighter note there is a musical 'Cabaret' evening, with tables, candlelight, drinks and nibbles, in a darkened school hall, held on two consecutive nights, usually in March. There is a 'Tudor Day' for the year-four children. This is one of the several 'living history days' on which both teachers and children come in costume, while all lessons and activities are set on an historic theme appropriate to the particular period the children have been studying. Through these special days, history receives a higher profile on the curriculum, while children and staff enjoy a diversion from the every day routine. The year-five children have an 'Egyptian Day' in the autumn term, and a 'Victorian Day' in the summer term. The warmer summer weather is also the occasion for the year-three children to don their togas for a 'Roman Day'. The residential school journeys also begin in the spring term: the first has left by the end of February, the last will be over only in June, in the summer term.

The summer term, which stretches through May into the last half of July, becomes in its final weeks one of the busiest times of the year. The term begins with the final INSET day of the year, and soon finds the children writing tests, years three, four and five taking the QCA (Qualification and Curriculum Authority) tests, followed by the year-six children writing their SATs (Statutory Assessment Tasks), the culmination of their work in junior school. With the latter out of the way, the year-six children can enjoy their week-long school journeys into Wales, while the year-three and year-five children enjoy Roman Day and Victorian Day respectively. 'Jump Rope for Heart' occurs in June, as does the return visit to Dollis by the Japanese School children. The first three weeks of July are the last of the school year, and are packed with activity. A 'New Parents Evening' offers an introduction to Dollis Junior School for the parents of children entering the school in the autumn, while a final open evening brings current parents into the classrooms for a 'celebration' of their children's work during the year. It is a chance to talk with teachers one last time, and to look over the year's work with your child. It is a popular occasion, and extremely well attended.

Sports feature prominently on the list of July activities. There are swimming galas for both the upper and the lower school, held at the nearby Copthall Pool, and this is also the month for a very special school event, sports day. For sports day, the whole school assembles on the back playing field, arranged according to their 'houses' (Pembroke, Garrick, Nicoll and Wilberforce), for an excellent afternoon of track and field events. There is a warm, enthusiastic and at times even electric atmosphere to this gathering, with lots of cheering and encouragement. The whole event is meticulously organised, with the headteacher's wife presenting the cup to the winning house, always to a rousing cheer from all present. It is an event which perhaps more than any other shows off the Dollis' spirit at its most expressive. It is well attended by parents, and is an event not to be missed!

In these final weeks music and drama too are also again to the fore, with a 'Summer Serenade' featuring a full programme of individual and group performances, and often a major upper-school production as well. If all of this isn't already rather a lot, there is also a school Summer Fête (similar in many ways to Fun Day) held in early July, every second year. By custom, on the Friday before the fête, the school sells candyfloss and, more recently, popcorn. The final weeks of the term are also an opportunity for class picnics, videos and games – and for the year-six children there is a special after school 'disco' in the school hall. The 'Closing Assembly' of the school year is done with special reference to the year-six children, who will be going on to secondary school in the autumn, and whose parents are invited to attend. It is customary on this occasion for some final words of advice from the headteacher, but also a last opportunity to sing favourite songs … and there is a chance to indulge in a bit of mischief by poking fun at teachers who have little choice but to grin and bear it, and won't be seeing you again next year!

Supplementing the year's regular schedule, are both special days and special weeks. The autumn term has been the occasion for a special week devoted to a particular aspect of the curriculum, or given over to a particular activity or interest. Over the past four years there has been a Science Week, an Art Week, a Local History Week, and most recently a Puzzle Week. Each is an occasion for special visitors and exhibits, and a wide range of activities, including some for both parents and children together. A Book Week held in April 2001 featured visits from childrens' authors (including Dollis's own Colin Dowland), writing competitions, and dressing up as a favourite book character. There are day visits by various groups and individuals, among them the Quantum Theatre, giving special science presentations. The Metropolitan Police are frequent visitors. In May 2002 they ran a Police Involvement Day at the school, with a variety of talks and presentations for all year groups. There have been workshops on Asian music, and on Shakespeare, while the Tudor and Victorian days are enlivened by the music and stories of Richard York. One special group of visitors to Dollis, in June 2000, were those grandparents who took up the school's invitation to attend a Grandparents' Day, enabling them to spend half a school day with their grandchildren. Special occasions at school have also been inspired by events happening beyond the school gates. In June 2002 the school organised two World Cup Football Match breakfasts, the children arriving at school at the unheard of time of 7.15 a.m., to watch the games on the large screen in the school hall. Earlier in the year the children watched the funeral of the Queen Mother. There have been occasional evening presentations for parents, to explain parts of the curriculum and how they are taught, specifically on the Government's recent changes to the teaching of literacy and numeracy. With the help and participation of parents, there has also been a series of 'curriculum and cultural evenings', each one aimed at a particular ethnic group within the school.

The year 2002, being both the fiftieth anniversary of the school and also the Queen's Golden Jubilee year, featured a number of unique events and visits. Foremost among the latter was an afternoon visit in February from HRH the Prince of Wales, described by the headteacher as the 'highlight' of his career, 'an incredible honour, an incredible privilege – a day of days'. The visit included meeting some of the staff and governors, a tour of the classrooms and an 'interview' by the children in the school hall. A special sixteen-page edition of *School News* reported fully on their (favourable) impressions! On 29 April the school held a fiftieth birthday assembly, complete with birthday cake, 550 jam doughnuts, and the children singing 'Happy Birthday dear Dollis Junior School'. In May there was a special whole-school photograph: 513 children, plus staff, clambered onto a specially erected stand to smile for the camera. In July there was a Golden Jubilee Fête, opened by celebrity footballer, and more recently Hollywood star, Vinnie Jones, a former pupil of the headteacher's previous school. Singer, and former Dollis pupil, Nicola Thomas of 'Pop Idol' fame, sang to the crowds as they perused the many stalls. There was a Jubilee balloon race, a miniature garden competition and an international costume parade. In addition to a long list of displays, games and raffles, the fête also featured a reunion gathering of former pupils, including some who had attended the first Dollis school during the war years, and one former teacher, Mr C. Thornton, from the early years of the new junior school. The Golden Jubilee Fête raised £10,000, which was a substantial contribution towards the school's fiftieth anniversary year fundraising target of '50 years : 50K'. Among the fundraising ideas was a sponsored walk and a 'Smartie Challenge' (filling a Smartie tube with coins). To mark the Queen's Jubilee itself, the school sold commemorative mugs and a CD of Dollis music and song. At the close of the year, at the end of November, a group of Dollis children took part in a special Jubilee tree-planting ceremony at Copthall.

A DAY AT DOLLIS

For Dave Hallett, the Dollis site manager, the school day begins shortly before 6.00 a.m., which in winter means well before dawn. Dave drives over from East Finchley, and about 5.45 a.m. begins the process of opening up the school. It is usually pretty uneventful, and a task little noted by others, save for one particular morning in October 1999 which landed Dave's early morning routine in the limelight of *School News*. Dave arrived to find the padlock on the main gates filled with 'superglue'. As the lock was unrelenting, and with his tool kit locked inside the school, Dave faced two immediate problems: how to get himself into the school, and how eventually to open the gates so that others could get in. Undaunted, the site manager solved his first problem by scaling the school gates (no mean feat!), and his second problem through the well directed blows of a hammer and chisel, which finally broke off the lock. The site manager became a celebrity in *School News*, and the incident serves as a reminder that school days are not always 'just routine' – ask any headteacher!

Indeed it is to the headteacher that we turn next, for while the site manager is busy unlocking the school, the headteacher is heading for the school, from Stanmore, by bicycle. He tries to be in school by 6.30 a.m., but often arrives earlier to get as much paperwork done as he can, before the day proper begins, with its meetings, phone calls, interruptions and inevitable incidents of one sort or another. From 7.00 a.m. onwards other staff members start to arrive. Maurice Markwell, one of the school's two senior teachers, is in next, about 7.05 a.m., having driven some forty-five miles from Buntingford in Hertfordshire, which is the longest daily journey made to the school. Maurice is also the longest serving teacher at Dollis, other than the headteacher, having started in September 1980, and apart from the headteacher and deputy headteacher, he has also the longest list of responsibilities, from the school pond to health and safety. About 7.10 a.m. Victoria Cleary, the kitchen manager, arrives, followed later by the school cook, Joan Murphy. Other kitchen staff will come later in the morning, but about 7.30 a.m. work starts on the preparation of some 500 school dinners, to be ready to serve at 12 noon, by which time the senior meal time supervisor and her staff will also have arrived.

By 7.15 a.m. the deputy headteacher has arrived, one of his first tasks is to be ready to receive calls from teachers unable to get to school because of illness or accident, and to make arrangements to cover the resulting absences – which can mean stepping in himself. From 7.30 a.m. the school is getting busier, more staff are arriving, and most will be in by 8.00 a.m. It is in fact a very busy time of the day. If there is a governors' committee meeting, its members will be arriving too – 7.30 a.m. for a premises or a finance committee meeting, 7.45 a.m. for the curriculum committee – all held in the headteacher's office. At 8.00 a.m. the deputy headteacher might be meeting with the senior management team; once all the staff and children have arrived, the day becomes increasingly less predictable for both the headteacher and the deputy headteacher, but once a week, on Thursday, at 11.00 a.m., they have a formal meeting together. Both the headteacher and the deputy headteacher also try each day to make several quick tours of the classrooms – whirlwind inspections dubbed 'one minute management'.

In the main stock room, the photocopier is at work on its first assignments, further along the corridor in the staff room, there are comings and goings as staff grab a coffee, and check the whiteboard for the day's special notices, and in the classrooms teachers are preparing for the arrival of their children. By 8.45 a.m. Kathryn Morrell, the school administrator, has arrived, and the school office is ready to receive calls and visitors.

Outside, beyond the office walls, there is a rising din of excited voices on the morning air. At 8.30 a.m. Carol Jeffery, the school welfare officer, takes post in the playgrounds. A few children (boys playing football) have been in the school grounds from 8.00 a.m. (some even before that), but from about 8.30 a.m. the number of children converging on the small gates leading into the upper playground (adjacent to Pursley Road) begins to increase, and from 8.40 a.m. onwards both playgrounds fill rapidly with children. As only one gate is open, there is a constant press of children. At the Pursley Road crossing, just by the gates, Dave Hallett is now wearing the coat and cap of a school crossing patrol, and with his portable 'stop' sign he assists parents and children across the road, which at this time of day is extremely busy, overcharged with an endless stream of traffic.

About 8.45 a.m. the deputy headteacher appears, followed by other teachers, and at 8.55 a.m. the school bell rings out across the playgrounds. The numerous games of tag and ball are brought to an abrupt end, and the din of voices falls silent. For the children the school day has now begun in earnest, and taking their signal from further swings of the bell, the children file into school by year groups. And as the playgrounds empty, the inevitable scatter of forgotten sweaters, bags and coats emerges, discarded regardless of weather, and invariably those of boys! These will have to be picked up and carried into school, to be deposited on the small mound of such things which resides outside Mrs Jeffery's school welfare office. The last arrivals scurry through the gate ahead of Mr Hallett, who then shuts and locks it fast. Those who don't arrive in time must seek admission via the school office – always with the chance of a reprimand.

Once the children have assembled in the classrooms, the first order of business is registration, after which, on Mondays, lessons begin, perhaps with the weekly spelling test. On Tuesdays, Wednesdays, Thursdays and Fridays, however, there is a morning assembly in the school hall. All classes are soon on the move, the corridors filling as each class proceeds in file to the hall where, in a miracle of compression, each class takes up its place cross-legged on the floor in a single rank facing the stage. Teachers and other staff arrange themselves on the chairs set against the walls.

Assemblies last from 9.10 a.m. to 9.30 a.m. On Fridays the assembly is devoted to singing practice, mostly hymns, and it lasts an additional five minutes. Having returned from an assembly, class lessons commence, usually one in literacy or in numeracy. At 10.35 a.m. the classrooms empty for a second time, the children heading out into the playgrounds for their first break and playtime. Some are carrying boxes containing games and sports equipment. Among other items, the school owns a giant chess set, donated by a parent. Children can bring their own skipping ropes, and tennis balls for games of catch. Those of the staff on playground duty are supported by the deputy headteacher, as often as he can get out, and the encouragement of good behaviour has in the past been further promoted by the presence of those children selected to be 'Buddies'. Distinguished by their yellow caps, the Buddies were on the look out to help others, offering friendship to children without playmates, who reported to the 'Friendship Stop'. Having been suspended for a time, the Buddies have just recently been reinstated, and are again to be a feature of the Dollis playground.

Fresh fruit is offered for sale at break times, and if it is a Tuesday morning, the school shop opens during the first break, courtesy of the school administrator, Miss Morrell, who is soon besieged in the small room which lies between the school office, and that of the headteacher, and which serves as 'the shop'. For sale are an assortment of pencils, pens, rubbers, glue sticks and folders, as well as T-shirts, ties, shoe bags and purse belts. Most recently a line of small and furry 'cuddlies' has been added to the stock – 'very popular' with the children! Breaktimes also offer another opportunity for the staff to use the copy equipment in the main stock room (resources room). At various times of the day it can become the busiest of workshops – the photocopier trawling back and forth, ejecting its paper copies with precision into waiting trays, the cutting boards, staplers and glue pots all fully employed, and over all, the rapid-fire clatter of the copy-printer. It is a natural meeting place, one for friendly encounters with colleagues, and often a scene of much activity. The morning playtime break is over at 10.55 a.m., and the children return to their classrooms for the final lessons of the morning.

As noon approaches, the kitchen staff sit down to have something to eat, and at 11.45 a.m. the senior meal time supervisor, Mrs Joyce Campbell, arrives, and about ten minutes later the rest of her staff. As the clock nears 12 noon all is ready for the midday lunch break. Pairs of class monitors, carrying baskets loaded with the lunch boxes of the sandwich eaters, make their way to the school hall, where the sandwich children will consume their repast while sitting cross-legged on the floor – or in good weather be allowed to sit outside at the tables in the Elsie Henderson Corner. At noon the corridors fill once more with children, Mrs Campbell directing the year groups as they come forward to the dining-hall doors. The deputy headteacher is present, too, often standing outside his small (very small!) office at the corner of the main cross-corridor and that leading to the entrance lobby – a very good vantage point! Vicky and her kitchen staff are soon busy serving the day's choices from 'the Yum Channel' menu, while two of Mrs Campbell's meal time supervisors keep order, perhaps also offering a word or two on dinner time decorum! The children go in by year groups, according to a rota, and all are to be out of the dining hall by 12.40 p.m., which can mean a very rushed meal if you are among the last to get a seat!

Some of the teachers will be having lunch in the dining hall, but others will be retrieving something from the refrigerator in the staff room, where a microwave oven is also available. On Fridays, however, every chair in the staff room will be taken as teachers crowd in for the weekly staff meeting, which starts at 12.30 p.m. Both the headteacher and the deputy headteacher are present, and for the next forty minutes a usually packed agenda is gone through at speed, with notices on everything from the monitoring of homework, to plans for Tudor Day, corridor displays, holiday days, and the state of the staff-room refrigerator!

The lunch break is an active time, not least for the many children who might have music lessons then, or clubs to attend – perhaps La Petite Ecole for some Français, or Laser Beams for a

Bible discussion, or even a short film. The playgrounds are also busy – another MTS is stationed at the doors into the lower playground, and others are outside, strategically placed, and easily visible in their luminescent yellow tabards, donned for the first time in the spring of 2002.

At 1.10 p.m. the lunch break is over, and the children reassemble in their classrooms for afternoon registration, followed by a quarter of an hour of ERIC (Everyone Reading in Class). The senior meal-time supervisor leaves promptly at 1.15 p.m., heading for Edgware where she works as a supervisor in Marks & Spencer. Some of the other MTS will have a meal in the dining hall before leaving, and most of the kitchen staff, except for Vicky, the manager, will be gone by 2.15 p.m.

On most days, lessons proper resume at 1.30 p.m., but on Mondays (during the autumn and spring terms) teachers and children gather in the school hall at 1.50pm to meet the Monday-afternoon visitor (MAV). At 2.30 p.m. there is a final quarter-of-an-hour playtime break, after which lessons continue until home time at 3.45 p.m. With their school day over the children are soon streaming out across the playgrounds heading for the small gates on Pursley Road, outside of which a crowd of parents and minders has gathered to await the appearance of their young charges. Among the crush outside the gates are the minders from Busy Bees, who will be taking some of the children into Canada Villa, where they will be kept busy until their parents come to retrieve them. Dave Hallett, once again in cap and bright yellow coat, mans the Pursley Road crossing, helping groups of children and parents safely across. In the playgrounds, teachers are out once more, this time to supervise the exodus. The deputy headteacher will have appeared, and possibly the headteacher as well, to help with the children and to be available for a few words with parents and minders. For some minutes the small gates (now both open) and the pavement are choked with parents and children. By about 4 p.m., apart from those children who are staying on for an after school activity (perhaps judo in the dining hall, or drama in the school hall), the final stragglers have reached the gates, after which Mr Hallett once again locks them.

Most of the children have gone, but the day is not yet over. As the children leave, the school cleaners appear promptly at 3.45 p.m., and for the next two hours they will be busy in classrooms and corridors, making certain that the school is always kept in a presentable state – an important contribution to the school's sense of self-esteem. Dave Hallett heads the cleaning team (all female), among whom are two of the school's teaching assistants. One of them, Julie Ashley, like many of the school's general support staff, wears several hats – at the moment she has three – as teaching assistant, librarian and member of the cleaning team. The work is done efficiently and well, and will have been further supplemented during the day by Dave who, never idle, is not infrequently found giving the corridor floors a once over with his industrial carpet cleaner.

For the teachers it is time to get down to marking, and to planning and preparing for future lessons. The headteacher, and the deputy headteacher too, will most likely be in their offices, perhaps seeing a parent, making phone calls … or getting on with the endless paperwork which constitutes no small part of school life. During the autumn and spring terms, on Thursdays, from 4.00 until 5.00 p.m., the teachers gather in the ICT suite for a series of 'twilight' training sessions, the format and subject matter of which are very similar to those of the INSET days. The school office staff have gone by 5.00 p.m. and the deputy headteacher tries to leave by 5.30 p.m. The cleaners leave by 5.45 p.m. Dave Hallett closes up the school about 6.00 p.m., but recently this task has been done by Julie Ashley, often closer to 7.00 p.m. There are always teaching staff who stay late – and yet may have further work to do at home as well. Some are always to be found still in their classrooms at 5.30 p.m., and a few after that – governors arriving from 6.30 p.m. onwards, for an evening meeting, have been known to see the occasional teacher still in the school.

On open evenings, and for school productions, the school doors remain open well beyond 6.00 p.m. As dusk turns to darkness, the lights of the school entrance lobby promise a warm welcome for all those attending. If for a school production or an open evening, the deputy headteacher, with a few chosen year-six pupil assistants, is always at the entrance lobby doors to welcome parents and children, and the headteacher will be close at hand. School productions and other evening entertainments are scheduled to begin at 7.00 p.m. (with performers expected to come about half-an-hour earlier), and may run as late as 9.00 p.m. before the final rounds of applause.

Dollis after dark is also the place and time for meetings of the governing body. There are three regular meetings (one each term) during the year, and an additional number of extraordinary ones as needed. The governors gather in the entrance lobby from 6.30 p.m. onwards, for nibbles, a coffee and a chat. Near 7.00 p.m. there is a sudden exodus as members vacate the lobby and head outside across the car park for the ICT suite, where Dave Hallett will have set out an open square of chairs and tables, the latter draped in red cloth, for the evening's meeting. Such meetings used to be held in the emptiness of the school hall but the opening of the ICT suite offered a new, and more intimate venue, which the governors have found to their liking. A warm, friendly and positive atmosphere pervades the meetings, not least because it is always good to hear how well your school is doing! Meetings are always well attended with very few absences. The deputy headteacher, though not a member of the governing body, has attended regularly, while periodically there are presentations from one of the teachers managing a particular area of the curriculum. The governors come together very much as friends as is evident in the aftermath of unexpectedly short meetings, which long after the night's business has been concluded, still finds the governors deep in conversation with each other. The chairman of governors, Ian Webster (and before him Steve Harrison), together with the headteacher move the meeting along at a good pace, while Miss Morrell keeps the minutes as clerk to the governing body. The whole is carried on with much good humour on all sides. Naturally enough the meetings vary in length, from a thirty-minute 'extraordinary meeting' to confirm the school's SATs targets, to two hours for a regular termly meeting. Clearing up and closing the school for the night, once the meeting has ended, falls as ever to Dave Hallett. He is the last to leave and will be the first to arrive the next morning.

THE DOLLIS WAY

There is in Dollis Junior School a very tangible, positive atmosphere, something often remarked upon by visitors. It can be sensed in the warmth of the everyday greetings between staff members, between the headteacher and the governors, and between the deputy headteacher and the parents. It is seen in the innumerable ways, and on the countless occasions on which staff, parents and governors join together in projects, from the smallest committees to the largest of school gatherings. The school's spirit can be felt in the unrestrained applause at a cabaret night, in the incessant cheering on sports day and in the warm and friendly atmosphere of a governors' meeting.

To describe a school or other organisation as a family may be a well worn cliché, but it is nevertheless one which aptly describes how the school feels about itself – and the Dollis family embraces both staff and governors, the children, their parents and grandparents, too. News of former pupils is always welcomed (and reported in *School News*), as are their visits to the school, especially if ready to tell stories of school life in the 'olden days'! A sense of continuity is important, and the school owes a great deal to the headteacher and to all those teachers and other members of staff who have given many years of service to the school. Dollis has always drawn the greatest number of its children from the immediate neighbourhood, and there are many families who have sent a succession of brothers and sisters to the school, and there are parents who were themselves once pupils. But the school is now more diverse than ever before, with many families new to the area, and from many different ethnic and social backgrounds. Yet the difficulties that might arise from so many different languages and cultural backgrounds, have been turned to positive account, the rich diversity of Dollis's children and their families becoming a distinctive feature of the greater Dollis family, an integral part of the school's identity. It is an aspect of Dollis life perhaps best epitomised by the appearance of the deputy headteacher in traditional Yoruba dress to host an African-Caribbean Curriculum Evening.

Dollis actively invites its children and their families to take part in every aspect of school life, and beyond the school's immediate family there is every effort made, especially by the headteacher, to develop the local community's interest in, and contact with, the school. All of this helps the school to raise money for its own projects, but the school for its part also makes a point of raising funds for various charities, both national and local.

Forging links with the wider community very naturally includes developing contacts with other local schools – in the first instance with the school's immediate neighbours, the Dollis Infant School and the Copthall School for girls. There are regular contacts between the headteachers, visits by individual staff members and by groups of children, while in the case of Copthall there is a regular programme through which Copthall girls come to Dollis to help the junior children with their maths and reading. The Copthall Hotpans steel band makes appearances at Dollis (many of the girls started playing at Dollis), while junior-school musicians perform at the infant school. The current headteacher of the infants, Miss M. McGoldrick, and the headteacher of Copthall School, Mrs L. Gadd, have both been Monday-afternoon visitors at Dollis Junior School. The staff of both the junior and the infant schools have enjoyed reciprocal school tours, while some of the junior school's Beacon money has been used to purchase two interactive electronic whiteboards for the Dollis Infant School. Further afield, Dollis's Beacon status has been used to great effect in multiplying the number of schools with which Dollis has regular contacts, and of course the exchange visits with the Japanese School in Acton are now of long standing. This wider exchange with other schools has become a further characteristic of Dollis Junior School life.

A strong sense of optimism pervades the school. 'Enthusiasm comes across from everyone … there's no feeling of fatigue in the place … the school is so happy, like a large family', were the impressions left with one recent visitor, Sarah Garwood, whose task was to assess Dollis for re-accreditation as an Investor in People. Nor is this sense of optimism an accident. It is an attitude taken from the headteacher, and further conveyed through the enthusiasm of the deputy headteacher. It is communicated both personally, and through the pages of the headteacher's weekly *School News*. From it stems high expectations for the conduct of both staff and children. In the words of Dollis's SENCO, Janice Rolnick, 'Raising Achievement is at the heart of everything we do at Dollis'. High expectations are greatly encouraged through the frequent public acknowledgement of attainments by both staff and children. The headteacher is quick to seize an opportunity for pointing out achievement, from complimenting children, seen in the corridor, on the smartness of their dress ('and be sure to tell your mother!'), to an on-the-spot decision to highlight an individual child's success in an activity outside of the school, in an assembly, and to hold this achievement up as 'a good use of one's time' – a theme found in *School News* as well. Nor is such notice from the headteacher confined to the efforts made by the children, for those of staff, governors and parents can win recognition. And the headteacher's example is contagious: others take up the idea too, with the result that there is a great deal of mutual encouragement.

The idea of being accredited as an Investor in People is taken seriously, and serves as a spur to be active in helping staff members to improve themselves, by attending courses or getting further experience relevant to their aspirations – 'would you be interested in the opportunity to attend courses in …', is a question always asked of newly appointed staff members. And the results are plain to see: many of the staff, both teaching and support staff, have obtained or are working towards further qualifications in their chosen field. Nor are others left out: for governors there can be new opportunities to attend a course, perhaps a chance to chair a meeting, work with teachers on a special committee, or be a member of an interview board.

Two Dollis institutions, *School News* and the Monday-afternoon visitor, have played a special part in creating and sustaining the school's unique ethos. *School News*, appearing every week without fail, has done much to establish a strong sense of community. The upbeat theme which runs through its many announcements, articles and various items plays an important role in encouraging effort and in setting high standards for both staff and children – and judging by their contributions, not a few parents too feel inspired to try a literary flourish or two in its pages, to organise a fundraising quiz night, or to put their particular expertise at the disposal of the school.

Many schools have occasional special visitors, but Dollis' Monday-afternoon visitor is something different, for it is a regular, weekly programme of special visitors, many of them prominent figures in their particular field of endeavour. They have come from all walks of life (and not a few different countries too), from business and commercial life, sports, entertainment, the arts, public life, the armed forces, and the legal and medical professions. And they come to Dollis, going 'through the famous red doors' (to quote one year-six reporter), into an assembly to meet and be interviewed by the headteacher and the children. It is an exceptional opportunity to learn something of what these people do and think, of how they got to the positions they hold, and what their practical tips for success are (for which they are *always* asked) – altogether an excellent mix of education, inspiration and positive advice.

The school sets high standards and has many awards attesting to its achievements. The children have obtained SATs results that are both above the national average, and well above those expected from schools of similar location and makeup to Dollis. These are visible measures of the school's success, yet they barely glimpse the full picture. The headteacher is justifiably proud of the 'value-added' to each child, as measured by the NFER (National Foundation for Educational Research) tests, which track the progress of each child between entry at year three and leaving at year six. By this measure the personal improvement of each child which passes through Dollis can be fairly described as 'remarkable'. Yet all of this still does not reveal everything, for there is a great deal of very good work and much learning done every week, by many children, which goes well beyond what is assigned, and which simply cannot be recorded through tests. High aspirations and achievement through hard work is a message which does get through to the children. It is evident in the effort that many children make to go beyond assigned class work, producing their own projects, diary records and models – and what better than to discuss them with the headteacher and see his report on your efforts in *School News*! And it is this evidence of extra effort, done from neither suggestion nor request by any teacher, that is perhaps the best indication of Dollis' true success, for it demonstrates that these children have been inspired, are seeking knowledge for its own sake, and are enjoying the pursuit.

The school has a very strong sense of itself and its achievements. Through the leadership of the headteacher and his deputy, the school has acquired a confident sense of accomplishment and a readiness to strive after further goals. Frequent visits from prominent people, Beacon status, a School Achievement Award, recognition as an Investor in People, the Quality Mark, the headteacher's OBE, and many other awards have fostered a special pride which is felt by all. The children, both individually and as part of a group, are always encouraged to be good ambassadors for Dollis, reminded that they represent the school wherever they go – and on school visits their good behaviour is often remarked upon. There is always a Dollis way of approaching everything – and to the deputy headteacher must be ascribed the verb form 'to Dollisize', meaning to shape or form in a manner both unique and appropriate to Dollis! Visitors are regularly impressed, and the compliments have been many. Sarah Greenwood, the Investor in People assessor, found Dollis Junior School to be, 'an exceptional organisation'.

Mary Rochester in the school kitchen, 1991. She retired in November after more than twenty years of service. All eight of her children attended Dollis.

Living history, 1940s. Andrew Spooner with year-six pupils, July 1995. (*Hendon Times*)

A visit from Richard York, year-four Tudor Day, April 2000.

Charlie and the Chocolate Factory,
February 1996. (*Hendon Times*)

Study trip to Mill Hill village.
Miss Haines' year-three class,
September 1998.

Colin Dowland with the Dollis
Deep Pans, Mill Hill Park,
summer 1999, just after returning
from Slovenia.

Go Nicholl! sports day, July 1999.

Waiting and watching, sports day, July 1999.

Year-three tunnel ball action, sports day, July 1999.

Right: The lap of honour for Wilberforce, sports day, July 1999.

Below: Skipping begins! Jump Rope for Heart, April 1999.

Summer Fête, 2002.

International dress parade,
Summer Fête, 2002.

Monday-afternoon visitor
Mike Gatting and children,
March 1995.

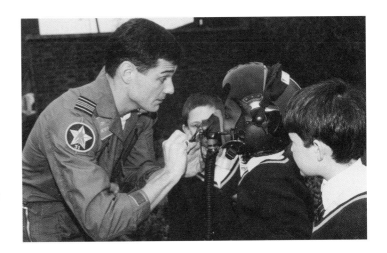

Monday-afternoon visitor
Squadron Leader John
Peters, January 1998.
(*Hendon Times*)

International connections.
A visit from the Minister of
Education from Singapore,
April 1998.

Investor in People! Raising
the flag, March 1997 (the
flagpole was a gift from Sir
Martin Laing).

HRH Prince Charles visits Miss Rita Alak's class, February 2002. (*Hendon Times*)

School reunion, Summer Fête, 2002. The headteacher chats with Mr Charles Thornton, who taught at Dollis from 1954 to 1967.

Japanese ambassador plants a Japanese maple to commemorate a ten-year association between Dollis Junior School and the Japanese School at Acton, June 2003. (*Hendon Times*)

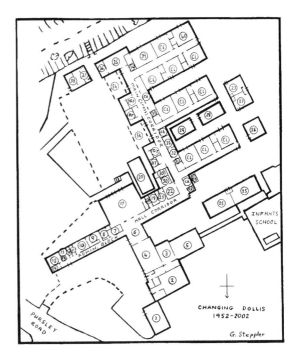

Changing Dollis, 1952–2002.
(See key pages 112–113)

CHANGING DOLLIS
1952 - 2002

1. Boiler house

2. Kitchen, 1952-1999
   ICT suite, 2000

3. Servery, 1952-1999
   Kitchen, 1999

4. Junior dining hall

5. Infants dining hall

6. Entrance lobby

7. School office, created in 1992. Originally a waiting space displaying team and club photographs. From 1979-1985 it was the Fiction Library.

8. Secretary's office, 1952-1992. Also used as a bursar's office. In 2004 became the school administrator's office. Used also for the school shop.

9. Headteacher's office, divided in half in 2003 to create a room for the director of strategy, this new room becoming a meeting room in 2004.

10. Resources room (photocopying etc.) created in 1984 from two "darkish stockrooms" which were originally a rest room and the senior mistress's office.

11. Men's washroom

12. Strong room/storage

13. Ladies' washroom

14. Shower room, originally the strong room for school records, cash, etc.

15. Staff room, has been used as a classroom in 1950s and a TV room in 1980s.

16. Staff office, created in 2002, originally a store room.

17. Assembly hall

18. Switch room

19. Medical and welfare room, used as a classroom 1966-1967.

20. Learner pool, 1969-1992. Elsie Henderson Corner created here in 1992, refurbished in 1998.

21. Originally a waiting space, it was used for a library up to 1961. From 1979-1985 it was a reading bay for less able readers, and later the school museum, 1999-2003. In 2004 converted into an enclosed room and used for musical instruction.

22. Music studio, originally a girls' lavatory and toilets. Altered in 1989 for a TV/video room, later becoming the music studio. In 2004 converted into a teaching room for small groups.

23. Deputy headteacher's office, created in 1993 from a girls' cloakroom. Acting assistant headteachers based here 2004-2005.

24. School greenhouse, 1988-2001.

25. HORSA hut classrooms, used by junior children, 1948-1993.

26. Music room, from 1974.

27. Demountable classrooms from Ravenscroft School, 1993.

28. Mobile classroom, 1968. Demolished 2004.

29. Mobile classroom, 1967, placed here in 1968. Served as a Reference Library, 1979-1985; Language Resources Room for remedial reading, 1985-1995; school museum, 1996-1997, and as a classroom before being demolished in 2004.

30. Pool changing rooms, built in 1975 in area of a disused play shelter. After closure of the pool they became a cloakroom and a storage room.

31. Site manager's room, originally the caretaker's storeroom

32. SEN teaching rooms, originally boys' cloakrooms. Converted into a central library in 1985, partitioned in 1995 for SEN rooms.

33. Cleaning cupboard. Cleaner store in 1952.

34. Kiln room since 1996, originally a store room. From 1978-1996 the kiln was in the adjacent class stock room.

35. New library, created in 1995 from a boys' cloakroom.

36. Food and technology room, opened in 1997, originally a boys' toilets.

37. Clay room and 38 Steel Pans' room. Originally opened in 1973 as a remedial reading centre. Partitioned in 1992, demolished in 2004. Central room was used for collection of jumble for bazaars and Fun Day.

39 One of two original "general purpose classrooms".

40 "Room 9". Originally one of two general purpose class-rooms, it was soon used as a regular classroom, but from 1961-1970 served as the library and projection room, also used for music and for listening to radio broadcasts. In 1964 a TV was installed, and it became a special science room as well. In what is now the corridor, adjacent to this room, there was originally a single large stock room (equipped with a sink) accessible from both the old corridor and from room 9. With the construction of additional classrooms in 1994-5 this old stock room disappeared, simply becoming part of the current corridor. The doorway between this old stock room and the old Room 9 became the current entrance to this classroom. The size of the original Room 9 was then reduced by creating three new stock rooms, to serve both this class room and the adjoining classroom, with the third stock room facing into the corridor—the entrance to this latter being the original entrance into the old Room 9.

CL – classroom
ck - cloakroom
GT – girls' washroom and toilets
BT – boys' washroom and toilets
Sh – outdoor play shelter

APPENDICES

APPENDIX 1

HEADTEACHERS

Dollis Council Junior and Infant School
Miss A.M. Willis 1939-1952

Dollis Junior School

Mr H. Bryant	1952-1963
Mr L.H. Patterson	1964-1978
Mr D.A. Heasman	1978-2003
Mr D. Burns	2003-2006 (acting headteacher and headteacher)
Mr C. Dowland	(acting headteacher 2006-2007) and headteacher 2007-

DEPUTY HEADTEACHERS

Mr C.N. Bissenden	1952 (chief assistant) appointed headteacher St Paul's C of E School
Miss A.N. Nicholls	Jan-March 1953 (chief assistant)
Mr Cleaton	1953

From October 1956 the local education authority established the post of deputy headteacher in group III schools (201 to 300 pupils) and above. The deputy headteacher was to receive a salary as a qualified teacher, with the addition of a deputy headteacher's allowance.

Mr A.R. Thorpe	April 1955 to April 1966 (died during the holidays; acting headteacher November-December 1963)
Mr P. Mulcaster	January 1967-July 1969 (appointed headteacher of Goldbeaters JMI)
Miss M. Collins	September 1969-March 1972 (appointed headteacher of St Johns CE School, Friern Barnet)
Mr P.H. Joy	April 1972-December 1980 (acting headteacher April-July 1978 and November 1979-July 1980)
Mr T. Bartlett	April 1981-December 1984 (appointed headteacher of Woodridge JMI, Southover, North Finchley)
Mr M. Markwell	(acting deputy headteacher) January-March 1985
Mr J. Betts	April-July 1985
Mrs C. Taylor	(acting deputy headteacher) September 1985-April 1986
Mr G. Lancaster	April 1986-April 1992 (appointed headteacher of Livingstone School, East Barnet)
Mr M. Heasman and Miss J. Henley	(acting deputy headteachers) April-July 1992
Mrs C. Livingstone	September 1992-December 1995 (appointed headteacher of Deansbrook Junior School)
Mr M. Heasman	(acting deputy headteacher January-May 1996) May 1996-July 2003 (appointed headteacher of Broadfields Junior School, Hemel Hempstead)

Mr S. Davies	(acting assistant headteacher) September 2003-July 2004
Miss E. Geeves	(acting assistant headteacher) September 2003-July 2004
Mr J. Preston	(acting assistant headteacher) from September 2004
Mr C. Dowland	(acting assistant headteacher) September 2004-February 2005; deputy headteacher March 2005-August 2006; acting headteacher September 2006-April 2007.

APPENDIX 2

THE DOLLIS TIMELINE

1867	Opening of the Edgware, Highgate & London Railway (Great Northern Railway), later the London & North Eastern Railway (LNER).
1898	Canada Villa built by George Wooley and named for his Canadian-born wife.
1905	Inglis Barracks opened as the depot for the Middlesex Regiment. Named after Lt-Col. William Inglis.
1930	Elm Farm is closed, and the farmhouse demolished two years later.
1935	Hendon Borough Council makes a compulsory purchase of 30 acres of farmland for its Dole Street Housing Scheme.
1936	Plans for the Dole Street Housing Scheme include an area set aside for construction of an elementary school.
1938	May – Construction of the Dole Street Council Junior and Infant School begins.
1939	Canada Villa converted into a youth club. 1 May – Dole Street (soon Dollis) Council Junior and Infant School opened. Official opening on 8 July, now named Dollis.
1943	July – work begins on a wartime day nursery, situated on Dole Street between Canada Villa and the air-raid shelters of the Dollis Council Junior and Infant School.
1944	March – the Dole Street Day Nursery is finished and ready for occupation. 3 August – Blast from a V-1 hit in the gardens of Bittacy Rise damages Canada Villa, the Dole Street Day Nursery and the Dollis Council Junior and Infant School.
1946	September – first civilian Road Patrol established on Dole Street bridge, to help Dollis school children.
1948	Completion of two prefabricated classrooms at the Dollis Council Junior and Infant School, under the HORSA scheme. Both are used by junior children.
1949	April – Middlesex County Council approves estimates for a new junior school on the Dollis site. Construction of Pursley Road finally completed.
1950	Spring – work on the new Dollis Junior School begins. The day nursery is demolished during the course of construction. September – Pursley Road declared a 'public highway'.
1951	Spring – remaining portion of Dole Street is closed off, allowing work on the new school's administration block. The new school is 'nearing completion'. 7 September – Mr Kitson's class of forty-eight junior children moves into a freshly finished classroom in the 'new school'. Building work continues. October – forced entry made into the new junior school building, and a further break-in in December.
1952	10 April – kitchen at Dollis Junior School opens to serve meals during the Easter holiday. 29 April – the new Dollis Junior School opens its doors as a separate school with its own headteacher, Mr H.E. Bryant. It has places for 320 children.
1953	2 June – Coronation of Elizabeth II. During Coronation Week, Dollis junior children put on a display of country dancing in the Hendon Schools Pageant. At Dollis there is an historical fancy dress parade and a film, using the school's new projector for the first time, and also a picnic. Ornamental trees are planted to mark the occasion. July – the new junior school holds its first Open Day for parents to see their children's' work.
1955	September – with 511 pupils on the school roll, the new junior school is 'filled to overflowing'. November – the first full inspection of Dollis Junior School finds it, '… a happy community in which the children were given every consideration and respond with great friendliness'.
1957	Summer – first Dollis Junior School 'school journey'. Forty-two fourth-year (final-year) children go by coach to the West Country for an eight-day excursion.
1958	Dollis Junior School football team win the Douglas Martin Cup.
1959	Football team win the Martin Cup for the second consecutive year. The swimming team came first in the Primary Schools Swimming Gala, and the cricket team win the final of the Junior Schools' Cricket Competition. September – 366 pupils on the school roll.
1962	The original Canada Villa is demolished and replaced by a new building of the same name. September – 322 pupils on the roll.
1963	31 October – Mr H.E. Bryant retires as headmaster of Dollis Junior School. Mr A.R. Thorpe stands in as acting headteacher.
1964	1 January – Mr L.H. Patterson commences as headteacher of Dollis Junior School. 320 pupils on the roll. A television set is acquired; it provides 'factual information on various subjects' and is, 'a stimulus for oral and written English'.

Football team wins the Northern League championship and are runners up in the All-Hendon Competition. The usual school journey is replaced for this year by day visits, including one to Coventry and another to Portsmouth. 17 July – official opening of Copthall Stadium, which is host to the All England Sports. Dollis Junior School used as a meals centre. September – 'Science' as a distinct subject is taught for the first time at Dollis.

1965 March – an open meeting resolves to form a parent/teacher association (PTA) at Dollis Junior School.

July – first meeting of the Managing Body for Group XI of the new Borough of Barnet's primary schools – includes Dollis Junior and Dollis Infant Schools, Courtland JMI and the Fairway JMI.

November – membership in PTA now consists of 204 parents, twelve friends of the school and thirteen teachers. By the end of the year, as a result of new housing at Inglis Barracks, children from service families start arriving at Dollis.

April – Mr A.R. Thorpe, deputy headteacher, dies after a heart attack during the holidays. Football team win the Martin Cup (Barnet West District).

1966 July – PTA sub-committee established to explore possibility of building a learner swimming pool at Dollis. In October the PTA decided to raise money for a pool.

September – 361 pupils on the roll. The medical room has to be used as a classroom. With erupting tiles in the hall, roof repairs, redecoration and an ever increasing roll, it is a very fraught term.

1967 Tracks lifted from old LNER line.

April – conifers planted on front lawn as memorial to Mr A.R. Thorpe. Football team won the Martin Cup.

June – Ministry of Defence to create a further 270 married quarters at Mill Hill over next three years – could produce need for up to 280 junior and infant places. Mobile classroom received and erected in future 'Elsie Henderson Corner.'

10 June – Summer Fayre makes profit of £529. Dollis takes first place at schools' swimming gala.

September – 373 pupils on roll, canteen in Canada Villa used as a classroom.

1968 20 June – fire in Dollis Infant School, children evacuated to the junior school hall.

September – 400 pupils on the roll. Another mobile classroom erected, between second and third-year corridors. The other mobile classroom is moved to the same location. Installation of oil-fired heating to replace use of hand-fired gas coke. Excavation of the swimming pool commences.

1969 3 May – official opening of Dollis Junior School training pool by the mayor of Barnet.

21 June – Summer Fayre opened by president of the Barnet Amateur Swimming Association.

September – 434 pupils on the roll.

1970 July – due to cost, the PTA committee recommends deferring indefinitely original plans for covering the swimming pool.

September – 452 pupils on the roll.

November – plans to convert the covered play shelter, adjoining the pool, into changing rooms are discussed with the borough's architect.

1971 Dollis ties for first place at schools' swimming gala.

1972 September – another mobile classroom, near the end of the year-two corridor, is acquired from the Infant school. (This became the music room in 1974.)

1973 February to April – an outbreak of dysentery requires buckets of disinfectant to be placed in all the toilets and wash rooms.

March – remedial reading centre is opened at Dollis, located in another mobile classroom erected at far corner of the lower playground.

21 March – NUT strike – Headteacher and nine other teachers on strike. Dollis girls take first place in Barnet West District Athletics.

November – Fuel Crisis, classroom temperatures fall to 49°F. Crisis continues into January.

1974 February – a magnolia, the gift of Mrs Meiklejohn, is planted in the school grounds in memory of Mrs S. Allen, who taught at Dollis from 1963-71. A weeping willow is also planted, a parting gift from Mrs Meiklejohn on her retirement after teaching at Dollis from 1963-73. Dollis girls take first place in Barnet West District Athletics.

Mr Leigh retires after seventeen years of teaching at Dollis, having, 'given freely of his own time in evenings and at weekends to conduct football and other sports activities'. He started at Dollis in September 1957.

1975 Easter – Aaron Stolow of Dollis Junior School becomes the Junior British Chess Champion in the under-ten age group.

June – construction of pool changing rooms commences.

July – Elsie Henderson is named Lollipop of the Year in a competition sponsored by the *Hendon Times*.

September – 380 pupils on the roll.

October – new changing rooms for the pool are completed.

Decorators, plumbers and roofing contractors on the premises; burst pipes, and a gale takes the roofing off four classrooms.

December – trees are planted 'on space between the kitchen window and Pursley Road' in memory of Mrs M. Hickman, deputy cook supervisor for eighteen years. She died in 1974. The money was raised by her colleagues.

1976 16 January – bomb scare at Dollis; children are evacuated. Football team share Martin Cup with Edgware.

June – first photocopier purchased for £102.65. Dollis girls take first place in Barnet West District athletics.

July – temperatures reach 100°F in the mobile classrooms. A class visit to Whipsnade is cut short because of the heat.

1977	Last (electric) Gestetner copying machine purchased for £201.09.

1977   Last (electric) Gestetner copying machine purchased for £201.09.

March – Mr Sowerby takes sixteen members of the orchestra on a four-day concert tour in Wales. Football team wins the Martin Cup.

July - Dollis Junior School is a 'reception school' for the English Schools Athletics Championships held at Copthall Stadium.

October – six silver birch trees planted, 'to commemorate the Silver Jubilee of the Queen and also of Dollis as a separate Junior School in this building'.

November – official opening of Copthall Pool.

1978   22 March – Mr L.H. Patterson retires after forty-five years of teaching, twenty-seven of them as a headteacher, of which the last fourteen years were at Dollis Junior School. Mr Peter Joy stands in as acting headteacher.

April – Mrs Dawon, school cook supervisor, retires after more than twenty years in the school kitchen. Dollis takes first place at the first schools' swimming gala held at the new Copthall Pool.

4 September – Mr D.A. Heasman commences as headteacher at Dollis Junior School and holds an introductory staff meeting.

20 September – the first Dollis 'newsletter' sets out the new headteacher's impressions of the school and his immediate aims. Red House Puffin Book Club starts at Dollis.

October – last AGM of the Dollis PTA; it is agreed to disband it. A new 'School Fund' is set up.

28 November – first annual Christmas Bazaar, held on a Tuesday, after school, makes a profit of £251.

1979   January – 327 pupils on the roll. 'Caretakers' strike', the headteacher and his wife (serving as temporary welfare assistant) take charge of opening and closing the school.

March – 'The Dollis Special' chartered train to York. The welfare assistant to operate from the medical room.

April – romance at Dollis; Mr Niblett, teaching at Dollis since 1972, marries Miss June Olney, a former Dollis pupil who, having left in 1967, returned as a teacher in 1978.

May – a new 'fiction library' is opened in the entrance-lobby waiting space. Pinboarding is put up in the school hall by parent volunteers. Displays can now be 'ongoing'.

4 May – a serious accident on Pursley Road, near the school gates, minutes before home time leaves three people injured. The incident led to protracted discussions over several years, involving Barnet, the GLC, the Department of Transport, and others, on how to improve safety. In July 1980 there was another serious accident involving a firetruck and a car. A single entrance for both the junior and infant schools was rejected, and a guard rail and crossing installed instead.

June – Mystery Coach Drive into Hertfordshire is put on for members of the local Darby and Joan Club. Mr and Mrs Heasman, with fifteen children, act as hosts.

July – a new single-sheet report replaces the old 'scholar's Report Book'.

November – a new central reference library is opened in spare mobile classroom, between second and third-year corridors. Dollis gets a colour television, and enters the police Panda Competition on road safety, for the first time.

November to July 1980 – Mr Heasman away due to illness. The deputy headteacher, Mr Peter Joy, serves as acting headteacher during his absence.

1980   Dollis swimmers win West Barnet District Swimming Shield.

Autumn – the schools' 'Managing Body' becomes a 'Governing Body'. The governors hold their first meeting on 19 November.

December – a Christmas post box is set up, with mail delivered by the senior-year children. The last of Mr Niblett's annual staff pantomime productions is performed.

1981   March – Dollis girls' badminton pairs finish first and second in Barnet Primary Schools Badminton Tournament.

April – football team wins the league cup trophy. Girls' netball team wins West Barnet Primary Schools Shield.

May – Mrs Pruski takes her first-year class overnight to Invinghoe. Dollis swimmers win the West Barnet District Swimming Shield.

July – Mr J.O. Blake retires after eleven years at Dollis, remembered for, 'teaching swimming and life saving to countless children'.

October – Mrs Heasman launches the first of many hyacinth-growing competitions.

December – last traditional evening carol concert, with choir and orchestra under Mr Sowerby; last candlelight carol service by Dollis children at the Free church.

1982   January – short trousers for boys no longer insisted upon as part of the school uniform (apart from the PE kit).

March – school drama club presented Roald Dahl's *Charlie and the Chocolate Factory*, admission 10p.

13 March – 'Book Event '82', includes visits from authors such as Leon Garfield. Girls netball team win West Barnet Primary schools shield for second consecutive year – a record! Dollis swimmers win West Barnet District Swimming Shield for the third consecutive year.

July – Dollis children line road to Inglis Barracks for the Queen's visit.

October – Mr H. Mason retires after sixteen years as caretaker of Dollis.

November – new 'thermal heat copier will be a major new resource for teachers', purchased from the School Fund.

December – *Christmas Magic*, the first whole-school 'Christmas entertainment'.

1983   March – Mrs Miller, a cleaner at Dollis for twenty-seven years, retires. Fir trees are planted at top end of upper playground along Pursley Road – the intention is to, 'screen the playground from Pursley Road and Canada Villa'.

19 March – 'Book Event '83' opened by Roald Dahl.

April – Mrs Shurmer's 'sponsored matchbox filling' raises £619.27 for the School Fund.

May – a BBC 'B' micro-computer, given to Dollis by the Department of Industry and Trade, becomes the school's first computer.

June – Dollis acquires its own book agents' licence. A break-time apple stall run by senior-year pupils opens during summer term – forerunner of the school's regular year-round fruit stall.

July – a management committee is set up to look after the new nature trail/reserve formed on part of the old railway line.

October – a second 'Dollis Special' train excursion to York enables the purchase of another BBC 'B' micro-computer.

December – 'The Christmas Music Hall'.

1984   January-February – a new 'resources room' is created in the administrative corridor by knocking down the wall between two small and 'darkish' stockrooms; paid for from the School Fund, work done by volunteers.

January – a record low of 269 children reported on the school's 'form 7' return. Tables and tray units begin to replace older desks.

31 January – Dollis parent and governor Alan Rockall's ten-mile sponsored walk, visiting ten local schools, raises money for Dollis Junior School, Dollis Infant School and Courtland School.

April – Mrs Nelms retires after thirteen years at Dollis, and presents two badminton cups to the school.

1 May – the NUT 'Industrial action' commences.

23 June – first of regular biennial Summer Fêtes is held, raising £3,000.

December – 'The Big Red Book'.

1985   February-March – a major breakdown in the heating system, with decorators and carpenters adding to the chaos created by the heating engineers. Dollis forced to close for two days in February.

26-28 March – strike action closes five out of twelve classes for three days.

October – a new library, created from the senior boys' cloakrooms in the main cross-corridor, is opened. Cost of £2,800 met from fête profits, work by volunteers. The old reference library is transferred from its hut, which now becomes the language resource centre, the new base for remedial reading.

10 October – first meeting of the new joint Governing Body for Dollis Junior and Infant schools. It includes an elected parent governor.

November – heating engineers begin a complete replacement of the school's heating pipes.

1986   Spring – NUT strike action finally ends. Dollis swimmers win the West Barnet District Swimming Shield.

June – Dollis inter-house swimming gala held for the first time in Copthall Pool. First playground seats ordered, paid for from School Fund, sponsored swim money and contributions from school leavers.

September – a fifteen-seater Renault Traffic minibus purchased for school journeys; a second was bought six months later. Introduction of ERIC – 'Everyone Reading in Class'.

December – pantomime, *Welcome Mr Whittington*. Corporal punishment in schools abolished.

1987   April – Mrs Webb retires after sixteen years of teaching at Dollis. 150 trees, mainly oak, hazel, elder and birch are planted in the nature reserve.

June – an officer from Inglis Barracks joins the governing body as an observer.

September – learner pool used for the last time.

14 September – Mr Bastin Surabi, talking about his school days in Tehran, is Dollis' first Monday-morning visitor. The second visitor was Mrs Patricia Heasman talking about her work as a practice sister in a group surgery.

December – *Cinderella – Belle of the Ball*.

1988   February – The Rumke family give a small greenhouse to Dollis, erected by Mr Lancaster and glazed by Mr Tom Barton, ex-school gardener, it is in full production growing tomatoes by May.

March – Dollis holds an open day which allows parents to see classes in action, sample the school dinners and attend a staff training session.

June – the school newsletter appears in a new A5 format, sponsored, printed and produced by Laing on Page Street.

July – Mrs Barbara Simons retires after a twenty-eight-year association with Dollis.

September – the school newsletter, re-christened *School News*, is to appear weekly, on Fridays.

December – advertisements begin to appear in *School News*. 'Christmas Music Hall'.

1989   January – a school shop is opened, with fixed opening times.

April – Dollis becomes one of eight schools in Barnet piloting the Local Management in Schools scheme, with a delegated budget of £300,000. Work commences on converting another cloakroom into a TV/video room, which subsequently serves as a 'music studio'.

June – Dollis takes delivery of 180 new polypropylene chairs, ninety 'ultra modern' desks and six storage units, thus completing the replacement of all the old desks and wooden chairs, begun '3 years ago'.

September – the year groups are re-designated as years three to six, instead of years one to four as used hitherto.

December – no production, postponed on account of Mr Lancaster's accident.

1990   April – new school tree logo appears for first time in *School News*. A motto, 'Growing Through Learning', is also adopted. Parents Dave and Sandy Young produced the final design. From September the new logo and motto appear regularly on *School News*.

May – volunteers organised by Mrs Wallace create a school pond between the year-five and year-six corridors.

May/June – Caretaker Gary Carney and his assistant, Danny Keane, remove internal walls in the HORSA hut, 'creating two "new" classrooms with nearly 50% more teaching area'.

September – Elsie Henderson retires after more than eighteen years as the Dollis crossing patrol. She had not been well and had not manned the crossing for some months. Dollis admits ninety-three children to year three, and opens a waiting list. A new school uniform is introduced – a bottle-green pullover with v-neck bordered by a yellow stripe, to be worn with shoes, not trainers.

December – *Oliver* and *Christmas Gold*.

1991   21 March – Toffee, the year-four guinea pig is re-captured underneath Mrs White's hut!

May – SATs (Standard Assessment Task) are written for the first time by seven-year-olds in England and Wales.

June – a seat and eight picnic benches are set up as a memorial to Elsie Henderson, who died in October 1990.

Summer term – year-three teachers and children dress up for a Victorian Day, the first of what would become Dollis' 'living history days'.

23 July – a special Prize Giving Concert is attended by the mayor of Barnet. The winners are chosen by the children.

December – *Aladdin* and *The Flight of the Bumblesnouts*.

1992   February – Mrs Barbara Peacock retires after twenty years in the school kitchen.

May – Football team wins the league title and the Martin Cup.

12 June – first visit to Dollis by children from the Japanese School, Acton.

July – a new school office created in the area of the old fiction library, the waiting space.

August – the school's learner pool demolished and the whole area block paved.

October – Elsie Henderson Corner, on the site of the old learner pool, is officially opened.

27 November – first visit by Dollis children to the Japanese School in Acton. They learn to 'wash' and 'mop' the classrooms, and enjoy an origami class.

December – *Snow White*.

1993   January – 360 pupils on the roll. A two-classroom hut arrives from Ravenscroft School. Originally intended for the infants, to replace two 'demountable classrooms' by the dining hall (erected in 1972), it is given to the junior school instead, in exchange for the HORSA hut, thus ending a forty-five-year occupancy by junior children of a 'temporary' building originally intended to last only fifteen years!

11 February to 3 March – ballot held to decide on grant maintained status – 64 per cent of the eligible parents voted. 186 were in favour, 159 against. The school's application was sent on to the Secretary of State.

April – football team wins the West Barnet District league, and shares the Martin Cup with St Josephs.

Summer – a new parking area constructed outside the school, doubling space available for teachers' cars.

1 September - Dollis Junior School becomes a self-governing, grant-maintained school. The joint caretakership of the infant and junior schools comes to an end, as Mr Gary Carney (resident caretaker of both since May 1988) becomes caretaker of the Dollis County Infant School only, and Mr Dave Hallett becomes the first non-resident caretaker with responsibility for the junior school only (commencing his duties in January 1994). The post of non-resident assistant caretaker is abolished, being no longer required. A thirteenth class is created in the junior school, and an office is created for the deputy headteacher at the junction of the main cross-corridor and the hall corridor – previously the deputy had no proper office.

October – Mrs Pam Isaacs, school secretary since 1978, retires. A new position of school administrator is created. The school holds its first Macmillan Nurses' Appeal Coffee Morning – 102 people attend, raising £230.73.

December – *Jungle Book*.

1994   February – the school acquires its first mobile phone, to be used by teachers in charge of school journeys.

10 February – year four dresses in style for its first Tudor Day.

March – introduction of the Singing Cup, to be awarded half-termly to the class which makes the best effort in hymn practice and during class singing lessons.

Football team wins the district league for the third consecutive year, and in May wins the league champions cup final.

21 March – Dollis holds its first Jump Rope for Heart, and raises £2,249.90 for the British Heart Foundation.

April – Dollis takes delivery of two Ford Transit fifteen-seater minibuses, to replace its first two. Work begins on three new brick classrooms to be added to the year-six corridor.

May – *O, Henry*, lower school production. Year-six children write pilot SATs in maths, English and science.

July – first Dollis Summer Serenade – extended in 1995 to a two-night performance.

October – work begins on constructing a new library in the old cloakroom at the end of the long corridor, near the entrance to the year-six corridor. Miss Caroline Paul leads the project, and has a computer installed which contains details of all the library's books.

November – Following a visit by the steel band from Aylward Comprehensive School, an order for a set of steel pans is placed through Mr Terry Noel, with a maker in Trinidad. The set to be paid for with money from the Christmas Bazaar.

December – *Wizard of Oz*.

1995   January – the three new classrooms in the year-six corridor are completed.

February – debut performance in the school hall by Mr Dowland, Mr Tivey, Miss Spooner, Miss Tuli and Miss Haffenden, on Dollis' new steel pans.

March – the new library opens (officially opened 4 April), the old library (opened in 1985) in the main cross-corridor is converted into two rooms for SEN use.

A lightning strike knocks out the heating boilers, but governors Colin Smith, Philip Colman and Steve Harrison turn up the next morning, 'with enough emergency heating for the school to remain open'.

May – football team plays in Black Cup final against Lavender School.

July – Mrs Betty Collis retires after nearly twenty-six years in the school kitchen.

December – *A Christmas Carol*.

1996 Dollis becomes the first school in north London to win the Investor in People Award.

January – 399 pupils on the roll. A tree planted in the school grounds to commemorate Samantha Karr winning the Watling Chase Community Forest Writing Competition. Completion of carpeting throughout the whole school.

26 January – visit by Mr Chris Woodhead, HMCI to unveil a plaque commemorating the school becoming self-governing.

February – *Charlie and the Chocolate Factory*. School museum set up in former language resources hut.

April – Dollis' first 'survey of parental opinion'.

May – senior choir records 'Songs for School Assemblies' with the BBC.

9 May – inaugural meeting of the children's school council.

June – OFSTED inspection finds Dollis to be, 'very popular, well led and successful … a very caring community which makes an outstanding contribution to pupils' personal development'.

October – Dollis holds its first 'No Bullies Here!' week. Newly christened 'Dollis Deep Pans' appear on ITV.

December – *The Lion, the Witch and the Wardrobe*.

1997 January – 422 pupils on the roll. A food and technology room officially opened by the store manager of Safeway, Queensbury, in room adjacent to the new library, formerly a boys' toilet.

May – *Cinderella*.

June – Dollis is top medal winner in the first London Primary Schools' Judo Championship – eight gold, nine silver and ten bronze. Dollis is awarded Barnet's 'Healthy Schools Initiative Award'.

September – a sixteenth class is created. Winner of a Grant Maintained Schools Award of Excellence.

December – *Oliver*.

1998 January – 454 pupils on roll.

March – acquisition of a Bosch dishwasher for the staff room puts an end to the staff washing-up rota!

19 March – four coach loads of supporters see the Dollis Junior football team win the prestigious London Schools' Black Cup under floodlights at Hornchurch FC stadium.

May – *Alice: The Musical*.

15 July – official opening of the refurbished Elsie Henderson Corner, part of the 'Playground 2000' project.

September – introduction of daily Literacy Hour, part of a new National Literacy Strategy.

1999 27 January – official opening of the school museum in a new location, outside the medical/welfare room, sponsored by the Midland Bank, Mill Hill, Broadway.

May – *Roald Dahl meets the Tudors*.

July – visit by Mr Chris Woodhead, HMCI., to unveil Investor in People re-accreditation plaque.

14 July – official dedication of the Adega Kalango memorial garden – in memory of a former pupil who died of leukaemia in 1997. Dollis Deep Pans visit Slovenia. Dollis Junior School is re-designated a foundation school. Rita Alak becomes the first advanced skills teacher in Barnet, one of the first thirty primary AS teachers in the country.

September – 'Home/School Agreement' introduced, as required by Government.

A refurbished, 'state of the art' kitchen is launched, with a new range of meals.

October – deputy headteacher Matthew Heasman introduces 'The Dollis Way' code of behaviour.

November – official opening of newly refurbished school library.

December – *Moving On*.

2000 January – introduction of a daily Numeracy Hour, part of the national numeracy strategy. 472 pupils on the roll.

February – OFSTED 'short' inspection finds Dollis '… a very successful school which is popular with parents and has a good reputation in the community which is well deserved … The school is excellently led by the headteacher and senior staff …'

March – new school pelican crossing on Pursley Road becomes operational.

June – *The Bumblesnouts Save the World*. Girls athletics team comes first overall at Copthall competition, and the relay team takes first place.

19 July – official opening of the Lea Caetano memorial garden, in memory of a pupil who had died very suddenly in September 1999.

September – appointment of the school's first part-time librarian, Mrs Sue Monti, followed in September 2001 by Mrs Diane Court.

October – New ICT suite in former kitchen area, 'ready for use'.

December – *The Twelve Days of Christmas*.

2001 Radio-controlled clocks installed throughout the school. Dollis receives a School Achievement Award, for substantially improved results over 1997-2000 period. Dollis accepts an invitation to become a Beacon School. Dollis is named a 'Gold Star School' in HMCI's annual report.

June – school governors hold a barbecue for the Dollis staff as a 'thank you' for making the school so successful; it is announced that the headteacher is to receive an OBE.

November – the school greenhouse, having been declared a safety risk since 1997 due to its thin glass, is reported 'derelict', to be removed immediately as a risk category '2'.

December – *Disney*.

2002 January – 505 pupils on the roll.

27 February – visit by HRH The Prince of Wales.

April – micro Librarian Fingerprint System installed in the school library

29 April – special assembly held to celebrate Dollis Junior School's 50th birthday – with 550 fresh jam doughnuts!

May – photograph taken in the playground of the whole school. Re-accredited as an Investor in People.

June – visit by Mr David Bell, newly appointed as HMCI.

6 July – Dollis Golden Jubilee Fête, featuring a reunion of former pupils and staff. First interactive whiteboard installed. New staff office created at the end of the administrative block corridor, adjacent to the staff room.

December – *The West End comes to Dollis*. Mrs Mary White, learning support teacher, retires after fourteen years at Dollis.

2003   January – 513 pupils on the roll. Dollis is awarded 'The Basic Skills Quality Mark'.

July – a power surge causes much damage to electrical equipment at Dollis; the damaged cable under Pursley Road is not repaired for more than a week. After fourteen years at Dollis, Matthew Heasman, the deputy headteacher leaves the school for a headship in Hertfordshire, and his father, Mr D.A. Heasman, resigns as headteacher of Dollis Junior School, having served in that post for twenty-five years.

APPENDIX 3

SOME MEMORIES OF DOLLIS JUNIOR SCHOOL IN THE 1950S BY MRS J. BOND (*NÉE* JENNIFER POWELL)

I was in the junior school from 1952-1956. I also attended the infant school.

I lived in Tithe Walk, Mill Hill. I just remember a quiet neighbourhood with few shops. Even then, the John Laing Company had offices on Page Street opposite the end of Pursley Road. I walked with friends through the fields to school, following the path, which extended from where Copthall Swimming Pool is now. I believe it went right to the school. We would amble home along the fields, playing and sometimes climbing trees! I don't remember parents worrying about the time we arrived home from school. It was a safe, happy place in which to spend our childhood. People from the surrounding streets knew each other well and used to visit each other frequently. I know that all the local neighbours would build a huge bonfire on 5 November and we had a glorious firework night, controlled only by adults. There was never any danger with fireworks as I recall. We played in the fields or on the street. In those days, there were many neighbourhood friends who lived on the same street but went to different schools in Hendon. I can still remember playing cricket and rounders on the road using the huge lamp posts as wickets or posts. We only had to stop the game occasionally for a passing car! We played out until quite late. I know we had some form of homework but I don't think there was very much. I also remember going for long cycle rides with friends during the holidays and staying out all day. We didn't phone home while we were out. It was always assumed that we would get home safely in time for tea!

I remember Mr Hedge, who was my teacher in year 5 (then year 3). He became quite an important figure in local education later on. I think he was a new young teacher when he taught our class and he was in charge of PE. He must have liked teaching because we seemed to enjoy the year and it was known that he was not too strict. In those days strict meant that children understood they had to do what they were told without question or punishments would follow, including having the cane or the slipper! I don't think Mr Hedge followed a curriculum exactly but we all seemed to learn okay. I think we did a lot of mental arithmetic and problems associated to pounds, shillings and pence. He also used to read to us at the end of the day. I remember he asked me which lesson I would like and when I replied 'games' there would be a huge cheer and we all ran out on to the field. Other teachers who taught our class were Miss Crewe, Miss Stirrup and Mr Kitson. There was a Miss Williams on the staff whom I believe had been at the school a long time. All the parents knew her well. Mr Bryant was the headmaster and Mr Thorpe the deputy head.

Our uniform was a green box pleat gymslip; a white blouse and a green cardigan. The tie was green and yellow. I think the boys wore grey knee length trousers with a white shirt and green pullover. I believe our shoes had to be brown with laces.

I think there was a choir and some children learned to play a few musical instruments. Many of us learned the recorder at school. There was a very strict teacher who may have been Miss Nicholls. She would watch us play and criticise constantly which discouraged us from learning. We had to practise on the stage. There were many of us there and Miss Nicholls would pick out children to play solo to check if mistakes were made which was so humiliating. I think I was in year 3 (then year 1) at the time. I had piano lessons at home, but didn't get very far. The teacher used to wrap us over the fingers if we got a note wrong. I think I was about eight years old and would hide when the teacher turned up at the house!

The dinner ladies were quite strict. I think we had to eat all our food before the table monitors collected plates. I seem to remember saying prayers before our meal. (We also said prayers at the end of the day.)

I remember doing needlework in the dining hall one afternoon a week. We enjoyed this, because we could chat to each other while sewing. I don't remember who the teacher was and I think she was generally quite strict but because she liked sewing her whole attitude to us changed for this lesson. It could have been Miss Nicholls. I think we learned embroidery in these sessions as well. Only girls did sewing but I don't know what lesson the boys had. It may have been something called craft, which involved making things.

It was a strict regime, but some teachers were more lenient than others. We dreaded going to the head master's room because this generally meant trouble. I was called to his office once because my brother had not done his homework. I was reprimanded for this and told that he must do his work. They seemed to be saying that I had to make sure the work was done. I thought this was grossly unfair and I couldn't understand why my parents were not told. I also remember that my brother had bronchitis and often coughed for most of the night. I thought it was amazing that he even went to school when he had a bad night. (I don't remember children being absent from school except if they had a childhood illness like chicken pox or measles). I know that my brother was 'given the slipper' on more than one occasion.

I think we accepted the regime in school but managed to enjoy ourselves. There was great excitement when the Hendon sports took place. We would practice for it throughout the summer. There was a long jump pit on the upper end of the field. Often we were allowed to practise long jump and high jump there, instead of attending class lessons. All the schools in the borough were closed for the Hendon sports, which took place on the field at the Burroughs. Everyone would attend to support the school. Local athletic trainers would be there looking for talent! I was lucky enough to be picked and had extra training which continued throughout secondary school. I think our trainer was a Mr Jennings who was well known in the area as an excellent coach for all athletic events. I spent many long happy evenings and weekends training.

We celebrated May Day when children would dance around the Maypole. This was a big celebration at that time. I think Miss Williams taught the children the dance. We also celebrated special days like Empire Day when we would all dress up in historical costumes and parade round the field. Teachers would judge which children received awards for the best costume. I think most parents attended these events. They went to a great deal of trouble to make costumes. In class we made maps of Great Britain, which were all coloured accurately.

I still recall the names of some of the friends in my class when I was ten years old. Some of these are named on the back of the photograph of the school netball team. We all seemed to get on very well. I remember break times when the class played rounders in the shelter – what is now the shelter where year 5 and 6 exit at break. We played with a tennis ball, which was often hit on to the top playground. I think there were some exceptionally 'clever' children in the class. I remember a Victor Tuffield and an Ian Hall. I think Ian went to the City of London School. I know it was a school where they wore long black gowns and we were all in awe of him going to this special school. All the girls in the class really liked those two boys. I think we played kiss chase on the field in year 6!

(Mrs Bond returned to Dollis Junior School as an advanced skills teacher in September 2003).

APPENDIX 4

SPLASH! THE DOLLIS POOL

One of the more surprising facts which a visitor to the school might be told, is that the present day Elsie Henderson Corner, with its solid tables and seats, once resounded to the excited cries of children in a swimming pool! The Dollis learner swimming pool was the creation of the old Dollis Junior Parent/Teacher association (PTA). In 1965, when the Dollis PTA was formed, there was considerable enthusiasm in many local primary schools for the creation of 'teaching pools'. Indeed the Hendon Head Teachers' Association had been pressing the local council for additional swimming facilities. At Dollis the aim of the new PTA was to build a pool that would allow every child to learn to swim at least 25 yards by the time they left the school. Following the example of other schools, the project was to be funded from voluntary contributions, with parents and staff also helping with the installation. The fashion for such pools in local schools can be traced to Broadfields Junior School where, in 1957, the headteacher, Mr McFarlane (1952-1969), first rallied his PTA to undertake such a project. Drawing on the example of a school in neighbouring Wembley, the Broadfields' pool was completed in 1959, and became the first such teaching pool in the former Borough of Hendon.

At Dollis, the plan as approved in 1968 by the school's Managing Body (predecessor of the current Governing Body) and the local council, was to build a pool in three phases, constructing first an open pool with filtration and chlorination plant, then covering the pool over, and finally in the last stage providing changing rooms. The estimated cost of the first phase was put as high as £3,600, against which the council would make a loan to cover part of the cost. To raise the necessary funds parents and pupils gave weekly sums, supplemented by the takings of jumble sales and 'a summer fayre'. With £2,000 raised, the project went ahead, supported by a loan of £1,000 from Barnet Council. After a number of setbacks, the first phase was completed and the pool officially opened by the Mayor of Barnet in 1969. But the original plan for a covered indoor pool was never to be realised, though the construction of changing rooms was approved in 1974. At the pool's opening in 1969 the mayor had announced that the council would be unable to finance the pool any further, which was in fact a re-statement of the position adopted as far back as 1967 by the former Middlesex County Council, when they opted for restricting PTA funded pools at primary schools 'to small open air unheated pools'. The decision had caused considerable irritation in Hendon at the time, but the Middlesex councillors were concerned over the ultimate cost of such projects, their ongoing maintenance and associated problems. Indeed it was concern over maintenance costs, hygiene and safety (particularly over the holidays) that ultimately sealed the fate of the Dollis pool.

The pool continued to operate into the 1980s, but there were always problems. The summer of 1986 was a good season, but it was almost the last. The pool was last used in the autumn of 1987. A final attempt was made to see if the pool could at last be covered over, but the idea was soon abandoned as the costs were prohibitive (at least £16,000). A serious breakdown in the electrical heating system and damage to the solar panels prevented swimming in the summer of 1988. Hopes that swimming might be resumed thereafter met with further disappointment, as they rested on completion of a new boiler room and heating system. In January 1990 severe gales destroyed the pool's wooden fencing. Vandalism continued to be a problem – the headteacher being liable if the intruders were to injure themselves! By March 1992 it had been decided that the pool would not be reopened. The cost of restoration was far too high, while nearby Copthall Pool (opened in 1977) offered an alternative for learners that had not been available when the Dollis pool had been built. Finally, in August 1992, the pool was demolished and the area block paved. For many it was a sad end, not least for staff who used to take the occasional dip after school! The pool's demise, however, made way for the Elsie Henderson Corner.

It is interesting to note that this small corner of the school's grounds has seen a greater variety of uses than any other. Once it was part of a farmyard. Subsequently it saw the presence of a wartime nursery, a mobile classroom and a swimming pool, before finally acquiring its picnic tables.

APPENDIX 5

SCHOOL DRESS AT DOLLIS

Green as a Dollis colour goes back to the very first days of the original school. On 9 May 1939, only days after the first school opened, the headmistress, Miss Willis, held a meeting with parents in the school hall at which a suitable 'school dress' was selected. In her log book Miss Willis noted down the decisions made. For the girls there was to be, 'a keep fit type of dress, no sleeves, green, with a buff sparva blouse – a wool material in winter, sparva for summer.' The boys were to wear, 'Grey shorts and socks, with sparva shirt or blouse … Pullover in winter. Cap, Green. Blazer, Green. Tie, Green, Brown & Buff.' The latter seems to have been a green tie, with widely spaced diagonal narrow buff stripes alternating with very narrow brown stripes edged in buff. Sadly, whatever uniformity was actually achieved, it was soon undermined by the war, which broke out four months later. Government regulations and rationing led to the suspension of a uniform dress, and it was not until May 1950 that it was again resolved (in further parent meetings with Miss Willis) that 'the school uniform should be worn again'.

Subsequently, as recalled by Charles Thornton, who taught at the new Dollis Junior School from 1954 to 1967, the rules on uniform were not strictly enforced. Nonetheless, when Mr Heasman became headteacher in September 1978 he ascribed much of the children's evident pride in their school to the insistence of the previous head, Mr Patterson (1964-1978), that children wear uniform … and that boys wear short trousers! Upon assuming the headship, Mr Heasman announced that one of his 'immediate aims' was to be the strict maintenance of school uniform, and though in July 1981 he was to declare that he had 'the total support of parents' in upholding 'the old fashioned tradition of school uniform', his insistence on short trousers for the boys was soon dropped. Caps and blazers were already a thing of the past, and from the spring of 1982 the boys were permitted to wear either short or long trousers. Previously, the only concession on the wearing of short trousers, had been to allow boys to travel to school in long trousers if the weather was 'cold', but only on the proviso that they change into short trousers before going into class! In allowing long trousers for boys, Mr Heasman declared himself to be, 'a great believer in all junior school boys wearing short grey trousers', observing that, 'Grubby knees are easier to clean than grubby long trousers and grazes on knees are less expensive than torn long trousers'. He bowed to the inevitable, he said, only, 'because it is becoming increasingly difficult to buy grey trousers for big boys', and as a result he was permitting all boys to wear either long or short grey trousers. It was certainly true that boys' shorts had become considerably shorter (and skimpier) than the more generous (and more becoming) cut of 1950. Short trousers lingered on at Dollis, but were gone by the close of the 1980s.

Dollis Junior School uniform in the 1980s consisted of a white or grey shirt, with grey trousers and a bottle-green pullover for boys, while the girls wore white blouses, bottle-green cardigans or pullovers, and bottle-green tunics or skirts. The school tie, now worn by both boys and girls, was green with yellow diagonal stripes, a pattern which seems to have been adopted in the 1950s. In winter a white or grey polo-neck pullover could be worn underneath the normal pullover or cardigan. In warmer weather, the boys were allowed to discard their pullovers, while the girls could wear 'green gingham or striped dresses'. Achieving the ideal, however, was a constant struggle, made no easier when many children were transients, and school photos reveal a variety of styles, shades of green, and an assortment of other colours, too.

A change, however, was on the way, and from September 1990 the school strove to improve its standard of dress, adopting a uniform consisting of a v-necked bottle-green pullover, with distinctive yellow trim, to be worn with the school's traditional green and yellow tie. Pupils were no longer to wear trainers, but to have proper leather shoes. The new pullover, with its yellow trim (obtainable from certain suppliers) enabled a transformation to a far more smartly dressed school, achieved over the following two years. From the autumn of 1992, all boys were to wear long grey trousers, a white or grey shirt, grey socks, black or brown shoes, a bottle-green school pullover trimmed with yellow (obtainable from Alfred's of Burnt Oak, or at Howard Bros, Mill Hill), and a school tie (available at the school's finance office). They were also to have a house T-shirt, white shorts, and plimsolls for PE. Girls were to appear in a bottle-green tunic, or dress, with white socks, a white blouse, a bottle-green school pullover with yellow trim and a school tie. Winter tights were to be bottle-green or black. The girls' PE kit was the same as for the boys.

The uniform established in 1990-92 brought a noticeable improvement in both the smartness and the uniformity of dress at Dollis, and was to remain virtually unchanged until the spring of 2002, when girls were permitted to add long grey trousers to their list of choices. White has become the only acceptable shirt colour, and along the way there have been occasional additional items according to fashion: in May 1997 Dollis Junior School baseball hats went on sale for £3 – to protect young scholars from the sun. School purse belts for girls have been sold at Dollis since January 1988 – 'smart and attractive'!

APPENDIX 6

THE SCHOOL UNIFORM
(SEPTEMBER 2002)

The school's outfitters are Howard Bros of Mill Hill, Broadway. Previously it was Alfred's in Burnt Oak.

Autumn and Spring Terms
Boys
White long-sleeved shirt (Howard Bros or chain store)
School tie (dark green with yellow diagonal stripes, obtainable from the school's shop)
Grey trousers (Howard Bros)
School pullover (dark green with 'v' neck trimmed in yellow)

Girls
White blouse (Howard Bros or chain store)
School tie (as for boys)
Bottle-green tunic or pleated skirt (Howard Bros)
Grey trousers (optional, from spring 2002, from Howard Bros)
Bottle-green or black tights
School pullover or cardigan (dark green with yellow trim)
Dark green purse belt with white metal clasp (optional, from school's shop)

Summer Term
Boys
As above, with white polo shirt optional for warmer weather

Girls
As above, with option of polo shirt in place of blouse
Summer dress of green/white stripes in place of tunic or shirt
(In practice green/white checked summer dresses also worn)
Available from chain stores.

PE kit (for both boys and girls)
White shorts and socks
T-shirt in House colours with Dollis logo on left breast in yellow (green for Wilberforce). T-shirts are red (Garrick), blue (Nicoll), yellow (Wilberforce) and green (Pembroke). These are obtainable from the school. In practice many T-shirts without the logo are worn
Pair of trainers and plimsolls
Tracksuits (any colour) for colder weather

Watches and jewellery are not permitted, except for ear studs

APPENDIX 7

SCHOOL CLUBS

October 1970
(Headteacher's report 22 October)

A 'tremendous amount of after-school activity voluntarily and enthusiastically undertaken through clubs for football, netball, badminton, agility, swimming, life-saving, dancing, music and chess'.

May 1975
(Headteacher's report 22 May)

Clubs – dancing, badminton and music meet regularly during lunch hour
Chess – sixty-eight members in the Chess Club
(Aaron Stolow became Junior British Chess Champion – under ten – during the Easter holiday)

September 1980
Activities run during lunch break or after school:

Netball
Chess
Recorders
Football
The Puffin Club
Orchestra
Badminton
Drama

April (Summer term) 1997
Lunch time:

Junior Choir
French Club
Fishes
Senior Choir
Chess
Recycling
Jazz Band
Nature Watch
Gymnastics
Recorders
Story Club
Steel Pans
Big Ideas

After school:

Library Club
Boys' Judo
Badminton
Dance
Girls' Judo
Athletics

During the school day:

Orchestra – Friday morning, 9:45 – 10.30 (by invitation only)
Composers – Monday afternoon, 2:30 – 2:45 (by invitation only)
Songwriters – Tuesday afternoon, 2:30 – 2:45 (by invitation only)

APPENDIX 8

SCHOOL NEWS

The Dollis *School News* began life in September 1978 as a one to two A4-page newsletter, run off on a Gestetner machine every one to two weeks, or as needed to inform parents. In March 1988 a first 'sponsored' edition (by Finchley Nurseries) appeared. Shortly after, Laing took up the sponsorship, undertaking its actual production, and from June 1988 the newsletter took on a new folded four-page A5 format, instead of A4 sheets, stapled. Having been briefly *The Dollis Junior School Newsletter* (March – July 1988), it emerged in September 1988 as *School News*, with a commitment by the headteacher to produce it weekly, to appear normally on Fridays. Detailed school journey reports become a regular feature, and the first detailed accounts of the Monday visitors begin to appear in 1989. By the end of 1995 an eight-page *School News* was a regular occurrence.

Typically, for the academic year 2001-2002, Mr Heasman produced thirty-eight issues, the last one appearing on the final day of the summer term. Through the generosity of Sir Martin Laing, the Laing company sponsored the Dollis *School News*, printing it every week at its Mill Hill building on Page Street. Pending the end of Laing's presence in Mill Hill, its sponsorship ended in July 2000, and from September of that year, *School News* was produced entirely within Dollis.

Over the years a strict weekly production schedule was adhered to. On Monday and Tuesday, items for inclusion in the *School News* would be typed up as they came into the headteacher, and on Tuesday afternoon he would start to put the whole together. From a table covered with papers, Mr Heasman, as editor and contributor, would pull together school notices and announcements, letters received from visitors to the school, literary contributions from different classes (and from staff and parents too), reports on school productions, school visits and journeys, and sift through the year-six reports on the Monday-afternoon visitors. Many of these items would have been actively commissioned by the headteacher, and in addition he would be writing up his own regular features: 'Time for a Chat', 'Something to talk about' and 'This Week's Quote'. Small advertisements from local businesses were also included regularly.

For as long as the printing of *School News* was done by Laing, the headteacher's 'copy' had to be ready for dispatch to Page Street on Thursday, the finished product returning on Friday for distribution to the children that afternoon at home time. When, from September 2000, the printing was done at Dollis, the task was taken on by Carol Jeffery using a copy-printer. The weekly printing of 740 copies was done on Wednesday afternoons, to be ready for folding the following morning (Thursday) by five parent volunteers, who assembled in the school dining hall for a coffee, a chat and a lot of folding! As Director of Strategy (from September 2003), Mr Heasman continued to produce *School News*, and although the schedule was altered to fit his new part-time working pattern, distribution to the children continued to be on Friday afternoons.

(With Mr Heasman's final departure from the school in July 2004, the production of *School News* ceased. It was replaced by the *Dollis Junior School Newsletter*, a single double-sided A4 sheet, edited by Colin Dowland, then acting assistant headteacher.)

APPENDIX 9

Some of Dollis Junior School's Monday-afternoon visitors, to 2003:

Gary Linekar	Sports personality and presenter
PC Peter Petts	Beat PC
Col. Mike Brown	Commandant Inglis Barracks
Tony Lambert	British Embassy in China
David Burrows	Chairman of the National Farmers' Union
Slom	Student from Moscow
Jyotsna Mehta	Headteacher from Bombay
James Grey	Mountaineer
Councillor Lesley Pym	Mayor of Barnet
John Personns	Mime artist
Sue Brooks	Help the Aged
Steve Theodorou	Professional photographer
Betty Blatt	With guide dog Worthy
Clive Herbert	Middlesex & Herts Wildlife Trust
Ralph Calder	Eighty-six-year-old Mill Hill resident
Richard Bryant	Architect
Charlie Stride	Black-cab taxi driver
Maj.-Gen. D.L. Burden CBE	Head of the Royal Logistics Corps
Dr Goolamali	Consultant dermatologist
The Drum Major of the Grenadier Guards	
Robert McKenny	Consultant orthopaedic surgeon
Terry Noel	Steel band player from Trinidad
Natasha Klugman	Actress and script writer
Gretchen Graf	Teacher from Montana, USA
Richard Burge	Director General of the Zoological Society of London
Catherine White	Professional harpist
Carol Rockman	Kite maker
John Redhead	Demolition contractor
Dr Malcolm McArthur	Pilot and medical missionary from Botswana
Mike Gatting	England cricketer
Tony White	Veterinary surgeon
John Peters	Squadron Leader RAF
Lisa Balson	British Airways cabin-crew director
Wilben Short	General manager of the Northern Line
Chris Spooner	Investment banker
Paul Brooks	Barrister
Lord MacLaurin of Knebworth	Chairman Vodafone and the ECB
Andrew Dismore	MP for Hendon
Richard Edgar	BBC and ITV weather presenter
Gareth Evans and Arthur Jeffrey	Chelsea pensioners
Lord Bernard Weatherill	Former speaker of the House of Commons
Justin Urguhart-Stewart	Corporate Director Barclays Stockbrokers

Professor Heinz Wolff	Scientist
His Honour Judge Dr Peter Jackson	The Crown Court of Southwark
Richard Quirk	Annunciator House of Commons & Yeoman of the Guard
Deka Salaad	Feature writer for *The Mirror*
Marjan Setnic	Slovenian Ambassador to London
Hugh Petrie	Barnet Heritage Officer
Lord David Puttnam	Film producer
Rt-Hon. The Lord Luce	Lord Chamberlain
David Bell	Her Majesty's Chief Inspector
Sir John Stevens	Commissioner of the Metropolis
Malcolm Chapman	Roller skating competitor
Michael Di Fiore	Restaurant manager, The Dorchester
Lieut. Gen. Sir Michael Willcocks	Gentleman usher of the Black Rod
Sir Terry Leahy	Chief executive officer Tesco
Sarah Price	International swimmer
Esmeralda Teo	Medical student
Robert Carpenter-Taylor	Beekeeper

APPENDIX 10

THE DOLLIS WAY (2002)

Do work hard	Do not waste your or other people's time
Do be gentle	Do not hurt anybody
Do be kind and helpful	Do not hurt people's feelings
Do look after property	Do not waste or damage things
Do listen to people	Do not interrupt
Do be honest	Do not cover up the truth

BIBLIOGRAPHY

London Borough of Barnet (Archives and Local Studies Centre)
  Borough (Hendon) Surveyor's Reports : Wartime Nurseries and Public Health committees, 1938-1953
  Minutes of the Hendon Education Committee, and related sub-committees, 1935-1965
  Decisions of the Education Committee, London Borough of Barnet, 1965-1995
  Mill Hill Historical Society, typescript notes

London Metropolitan Archives
  Middlesex County Council – reports of various committees, 1946-1956
  Middlesex County Council – minutes of Sites and Buildings Sub-Committee (Education), 1948-1952

The National Archives (Public Record Office)
  Ministry of Education, reports by HM Inspectors, ED 156/144

Dollis Infant School
  Log book, Dollis Council Junior and Infant School, 1939-1946
  Log book, Dollis Council Junior and Infant School, 1946-1951
  Stock and Stores Account, 1939-1949
  Stock and Stores Account, 1949-1952
  Stock and Stores Account, 1952-1955
  Inventory Book, 1955-1972

Dollis Junior School
  Plans, c.1949-1951
  Inventory Book, 1952-1978
  Log Book, Dollis Junior School, 1964-1971
  Log Book, Dollis Junior School, 1971-1978
  Log Book, Dollis Junior School, 1978-1981
  School Admission Register, 1964-1978
  Staff notices, 1978-1986
  School notices and sundry papers, 1978-1986
  School notices and sundry papers, 1998-2003
  Headteachers' reports (Dollis Junior and Infants' School, and Dollis Junior School), 1947-1986
  Reports of Governors' meetings (group 11 governing body and governing body for Dollis Junior
  and Dollis Infants schools), 1982-1986
  Reports of Governors' meetings, with sundry supporting papers, etc, 1978-1987
  Correspondence (headteacher, Dollis Junior School, with Barnet education services), 1985-1986
  Headteacher's reports for governors' meetings, 1999-2003
  School Improvement Plan, 2002-2003
  OFSTED, inspection report, 7-9 Feb 2003
  OFSTED, 2000 Panda Report for Dollis Junior School
  School Newsletter, 1978-1988
  School News, 1988-2004
  '50 wonderful years', some reflections, by Derek Heasman, (extracted from *School News*, 2004)

Ralph Calder, *Mill Hill: A Thousand Years of History* (1993)
John Hopkin, *A History of Hendon* (1964)